A Concise New
Training Method

GAME
DOG

The Hunter's Retriever for Upland Birds and Waterfowl

Second Edition

RICHARD A. WOLTERS
Author of Water Dog and Gun Dog

Foreword by Dave Meisner
Editor and Publisher
The Pointing Dog Journal

Epilogue by Gene Hill
Photography by Dale Spartas

 A DUTTON BOOK

DUTTON
Published by the Penguin Group
Penguin Books USA Inc., 375 Hudson Street,
New York, New York 10014, U.S.A.
Penguin Books Ltd, 27 Wrights Lane,
London W8 5TZ, England
Penguin Books Australia Ltd, Ringwood,
Victoria, Australia
Penguin Books Canada Ltd, 10 Alcorn Avenue,
Toronto, Ontario, Canada M4V 3B2
Penguin Books (N.Z.) Ltd, 182–190 Wairau Road,
Auckland 10, New Zealand

Penguin Books Ltd, Registered Offices:
Harmondsworth, Middlesex, England

First published by Dutton, an imprint of Dutton Signet,
a division of Penguin Books USA Inc.
Distributed in Canada by McClelland & Stewart Inc.

First Printing, December, 1983
First Printing, Second Edition, January, 1995
20 19 18 17 16 15

REGISTERED TRADEMARK—MARCA REGISTRADA

All photographs by Dale Spartas except:
    Pages 35, 39, 68, 69, Andre Pennard; pages 66, 67, Mary Sue Sweeney; pages 148, 149,
    Dave Krammerer; pages 152 *(top)*, 153, 171, 174, 175, Dave Follensbee; pages 5, 16, 18, 25, 26,
    45–49, 52, 56, 100, 105, 106, 133, 155, 183, and endpapers, Richard A. Wolters.
Diagrams by Gretchen D'Beck.

LIBRARY OF CONGRESS CATALOGING-IN-PUBLICATION DATA:

Wolters, Richard A.
  Game Dog.

  1. Retrievers. 2. Dogs—Training. I. Title.
SF429.R4W597 1983   636.7'0886   83-7196

ISBN 0-525-93942-3

Printed in the United States of America

Dedicated . . . to My Buddy

Young Tar is the hero of this book but the dedication goes to his older friend, Jet. Jet was almost five when Tar came to join us in the big kennel. Only once did Jet scold the pup, and that happened the first night when they had their dinner. Pup wanted grown-up food and Jet told him no. Never "ag'in" did the youngster try to steal from Jet's dish. But they both developed a habit that said much about their short life together. The first to finish dinner sat and waited for the other, then they would circle and switch pans, hoping a crumb might have been overlooked. They started as friends and in that year they lived together they never had a cross bark except for that first evening.

Since Jet came to me first, he was taught to heel on my left. Tar's place was on my right, and they learned to work from their own side one at a time and never begrudged each other his turn. They were real pals. In the beginning Jet took the role of mother, then as Tar grew he became big brother. . . . Oh, how they romped and played, but when it came to work they could not be beaten. Jet was a marvelous hunter.

Jet was a workaholic in the field . . . loved goose hunting on the Eastern Shore and had the drive of a springer on upland birds. But besides that, what a gentleman he was in public! I have to smile when I think of the time we were invited to be a part of a convention in Philadelphia. Booked at the headquarters, the elegant Belview Stratford hotel, where no dogs were allowed, I put on black glasses and lived for four days in the hotel as a blind man. It wasn't easy, and in my absentminded way nearly a disaster. Example: I forgot and left my reading glasses hanging on a string around my neck, while fumbling in public in my black "blind man" glasses. It took me time to learn how to play my role, but not Jet. He carried off his end of the deal with style, leading me everywhere, up and down steps, around revolving doors, even into the dining room. The doorman gave him a pat every morning and remarked how well trained he was to do his job. He was better behaved in the bar than most of the guests. Then there was the story in Atlanta . . . the same thing again—no dogs were permitted at a cocktail party in the ballroom of the Omni Hotel. We arrived and pretty women fussed over Jet—not me—and a waiter brought him roast beef—prime, rare! What a rhubarb that caused with security people and managers! It took the guest of honor, the Undersecretary of the Interior of the United States, to convince the management that if his invited guest, friend Jet, was not included at the private party, the function would be canceled immediately and they could send their waiters home. A hundred and fifty people clapped with glee as the undersecretary announced, "No one will discriminate against my invited guests because of color. My friend Jet will stay!"

Jet was the backbone of my retriever-training courses for the hunter, sponsored by the Orvis Company. I am only as good as my dogs. The students applauded his work. On our last lecture tour he got rave reviews on the evening news. He was a ham whether in class, on TV, leading the "blind," or in the hunting field . . . he loved his life's work.

Jet, Tar, and I flew all over the country together—young Tar was learning the ropes. A short while ago we went to Houston to teach our course, where Jet demonstrated my ideas in his usual fine style, and then on to San Antonio to lecture. The last day of the trip I noted that Jet was a little lethargic—too much flying or a water change? When we came home he did not eat, didn't touch his food, and even Tar was concerned and confused. There was no one for him to romp with, no empty pan for Tar to circle and lick. . . . Cancer works fast!

On the evening of the fourth day, Jet and I walked alone in the veterinarian's yard and we talked and I held him very close. I reminded him of the cold day hunting on the sound where I almost froze to death and he was bored without any birds, so he broke the ice just to swim. . . . He nuzzled unsteadily against my leg and it brought tears, . . . but we laughed about the time he flushed a pheasant and after he made the retrieve I couldn't get him to come on and continue hunting. He wanted back and kept fussing at the old smells at the same spot. Displeased, I went on and left him. . . . In a few minutes he was at my side, looking up, delivering a fat ringneck, his wagging tail saying, "Trust me, Boss." We had much to say that crisp, starlit evening in March—and so little time. The hour was late and the vet had to go home to supper. It should have been Jet's suppertime too. I was angry, confused. I wanted more time to walk and talk with my buddy . . . he was only five, there should have been many more seasons together. Life had to go on—but, in Jet's case, life had to stop.

Two days later young Tar and I were in California teaching. A blind retrieve was set up. With no dog now at my left side and only a youngster on my right, we went to work. I heeled Tar and sat him so he was directed toward the blind—a duck hidden 150 yards out by that big acacia tree. I leaned over very, very close to him, my hand in front of his massive head, pointing the way. His whole body quivered; he was ready to go! I held him there an extra long time to be sure he knew the exact direction I wanted him to run. Actually he did not need the extra time, and I knew that. What the class did not know was that I was telling him in a whisper that I thought Jet might be over behind the big tree and if he got into trouble . . . to go there and Jet would help him find the bird.

Friday night,
March 18, 1983

7

A Thought About This Book

As the author of this retriever-training book I hope that it will be nicknamed "the Hunter's Book." From the moment this book was conceived it was planned to be small—or better yet, concise—and aimed directly at the hunter. A lot has been written on the subject of retriever training over the past century and a half, and original thinking is hard to come by. This accumulation written mostly for the field trialer, not the hunter, does become a problem. So much has been written, in fact, there are so many ways for the hunter to go, that it has presented a confused issue for him. This book is to "unconfuse" the hunter and his dog. The 150 years that have gone before us have been my problem to wade through. This book is designed to fill only the hunter's needs, with all the extraneous material eliminated. It's a step-by-step, logical procedure gathered from the old and new information alike. It starts at the beginning—and you will see that the early months are vitally important—and ends with a dog that will do everything required in the field. If the step-by-step plan is followed—and it is short and direct—success is guaranteed.

We have eliminated many of the old wives' tales about dog training and taken out the material that the field trainer uses but that is not important to the hunter. We have added a number of instructions that are important for the hunter's dog but that have never before appeared in training literature.

Some thirty years ago I wrote *Water Dog* and used a great dog. Tar, to show the reader the way. That name was brought out of retirement. The real name of the dog used in this book is Tartu, shortened to Tar . . . he's got a lot to live up to and seems to be doing it.

Both dog and master owe an indirect thanks to *Gun Dog* magazine. Two things brought the idea for this book to mind. The overwhelming response to my magazine columns on the Hunting Retriever Stake showed just how many people out there wanted information on hunter training for their dogs. The stake procedures discussed in Chapter 8 first appeared in the magazine. The other "happening" took place in my study while writing one of my columns. I wrote that no book has been written on retriever training directly for the upland bird and waterfowl hunter. I stopped and looked at that . . . read it again, and decided to do this book.

Tar and I have done our best to make this book for the hunter a working gem.

Contents

Foreword

I came face to face with Richard A. Wolters for the first time in 1981 at a hunt club in the Northeast. I'd arranged the meeting because I was anxious to get his advice, comments, and suggestions concerning the impending launch of my new publication, *Gun Dog* magazine. After all, I'd more or less stolen the title from Dick's first book, and I felt that his input would be appropriate and could be important. As always, Dick's black Labrador had traveled with him, and Jet sat in on most of our meetings.

Our discussions were fruitful, and I came away not only with a lot of good advice but with a regular department editor as well; Dick served as my retriever columnist until I sold *Gun Dog* in 1985. It was while writing his regular bimonthly column for me that he came up with the idea of practical tests for hunting retrievers—and NAHRA was conceived.

After we'd concluded our business, we were informed of an advanced retriever training seminar being held nearby. We decided to attend for a while as spectators. When we arrived at the scene, Dick was introduced to the trainer conducting the seminar. As was usually the case, Wolter's reputation had proceeded him. His unconventional training methods and their striking success always baffled many of the professional dog trainers reared on more conventional methods. The trainer, with an "I'll-show-you" sneer on his face, turned to the dozen or so experienced hunters in his class and sarcastically announced, "Well, guys, look what we've got here. It's the one and only Richard A. Wolters—the man who wrote *the* book!" Then, he challenged Dick to "show us how it's supposed to be done."

I cringed. Dick had come up for a business meeting, not an advanced training seminar. His dog was "cold," and he was being put in a heck of a spot. I was sure he couldn't possibly be prepared for this.

As it turned out, there was no need for my concern. I learned then, and saw on many other occasions, that Richard A. Wolters was *always* prepared. Undaunted, he nonchalantly walked to the line and, in his own inimitable fashion, put Jet through a demonstration bordering on perfection. I was impressed, the seminar attendees were amazed, and the old pro ate his humble pie and asked Dick to help with the rest of the seminar. Wolters and Jet hammered their way through the whole thing, enjoying their work and taking it all in stride. Later, as I watched Dick work with the other handlers and their dogs, there was no question in my mind that this was a man who knew what he was talking about and was very well prepared indeed.

Dick Wolters was already well prepared in 1961 when he sat down and wrote *Gun Dog*, a book that took the wind out of the sails of many of the old-line, hard-core trainers, with revolutionary new training schedules and techniques that really worked.

He was prepared when *Water Dog, Family Dog, City Dog*, and all the rest followed, and especially well prepared in 1981 when, after 20,000 miles of travel and two years of research, he wrote *The Labrador Retriever: The History . . . the People*, which won the Dog Writers Association Book of the Year.

And again, Dick demonstrated his preparedness, his knowledge, his insight into what was needed by writing the first edition of this book—perhaps his most significant contribution—in 1983. Dick believed that hunters with retrievers were the most neglected segment of the dog-owning populace. Ironically, while retriever field trailers represent a minuscule percentage of retriever owners, almost every retriever training book written before *Game Dog* concentrated on trialers' methods. To be sure, a few training books touched on training the hunter's retriever, but *Game Dog* was the first book devoted totally and exclusively to training retrievers for upland bird and waterfowl hunting.

The everyday hunter and his dog lost a great champion when Dick died on October 9, 1993. In my mind, he did more for the hunter with a retriever than anyone else in history. And while he was known best for his work with retrievers, those of us who shoot over pointing dogs owe him a huge debt of gratitude as well. *Gun Dog*, his first major dog book, has helped literally hundreds of thousands of pointing dog owners train their dogs.

Richard A. Wolters was a truly remarkable and unforgettable character, boisterous and cantankerous on the outside, sensitive on the inside, with a heart as big as the outdoors he loved. Watch how a man's dog feels about him, and you'll know a lot about the man. On numerous occasions, I watched Dick put his dogs through their paces, and I know how they—with every fiber of their being—worshipped him and wanted to please him. In the epilogue to this book Gene Hill writes about Wolters, "When a man is proud of his dog and shows it, I like him. When his dog is proud of him and shows it, I deeply respect him." Me, too, Gene.

Richard A. Wolters. He is missed.

DAVE MEISNER
The Pointing Dog Journal
Adel, Iowa
June 1994

Chapter 1

Setting the Stage

WHY THIS BOOK?

If your main interest in retrievers is for field trials take this book back to the bookstore and ask for a refund. This is the first dog-training book especially for both the upland bird and the waterfowl hunter, and it is like no other book in its field.

As we go along, you will see that I am certainly not against field trials. On the contrary, field trials play an important role in shaping today's retrievers. If it were not for field trials, we would most likely have lost our dog by this time. Any time a breed becomes popular with the general public, its original purpose seems to get lost. The only feathers most Labradors and Goldens see today are on the hatbands of their mistresses. Retriever trials, a very special game that has been going on for fifty years in this country and for more than eighty in England, have kept the "work" in the breed.

Browsing through the dog literature, you will find that the books follow two main streams . . . the breed books written by the show people and the training books written by those who trial. Some might claim that this is not so, but on close examination of the training books used by the hunter you will find that nearly always the philosophy behind them is definitely for field trials. This will become clear as we go on. There is a scarcity in the literature exclusively for the hunter. Why has so little been written expressly for him? Because the people who have written the training books are serious about their training, and they happen to be field-trial oriented.

Look at it this way. There are three groups interested in our retrievers: the show people, the field trialers, and the hunters. The first two are well organized into national groups and have specific goals. No book that has been written by a show person has any value for the hunter as far as training is concerned. Books by field trialers serve to supplement the training that takes place in the club, or to help the beginner. Some books written by them are designed for the advanced trialer. Where does the hunter come off in all of this? He plays a different game locally with his cronies. There are few avenues of communication between hunters of different areas, and so they play their sports differently in different parts of the country. In field-trial clubs, people learn by seeing other club members handle their dogs. They watch advanced dogs do their jobs and, by so doing, see what they have to work toward. Many hunters, on the other hand, never see a good dog work.

So hunters, who outnumber the trial and show people by hundreds of thousands, are at a real disadvantage. Having little or no chance to see really good dogs work, many hunters do not realize the dog's potential. They have little understanding of what it takes to train and handle a dog, and yet it is a very simple procedure. Most hunters even have trouble when it comes time to start a new pup. If their local cronies' dogs are not having pups, they don't even know where to go to get working stock. That's one of the great advantages the field trialers have. They'll know who the best dogs are, can readily make arrangements for breeding, and ship pups all over the country.

But there is an even bigger problem the hunter has to face. Working a dog up through the ranks in field trials requires precision training. A finished trial dog is one of the world's most sophisticated animals. Such sophistication is much more than the hunter needs. Because the basic philosophy behind all the training books is that of the field trial, most hunters get lost after page 30. It's not that they don't understand what they are reading, it's mainly the fact that this "college" education requires more time, work, and money than they want to put into it.

By tradition the hunter feels he wants a good dog to be his pal and co-worker in the field. Gene Hill, with all his grand writing and dog stories, has convinced the hunter that he needs a fine dog to lie curled at his feet in front of the fireplace while he reads Gene's nostalgic hunting yarns. But Gene does not tell how to make that pal into a fine hunter.

If one takes a moment to examine the situation, he finds that the field-trial and show people are dedicated to their dogs and spend all their free time actively pursuing the dog game. Often their entire social life revolves around other doggy people. But most hunters do their thing for only a few months in the fall and although their dog is important to them, their major interest is not in their dogs but in their guns and the game.

But there is a way around all of this. First, the hunter must know what kind of hunting he is going to do. Once he decides that, the training of his dog will be directed to that end. In some areas we shall be shortcutting the education of the dog and shall teach him *from the beginning* those things that will answer the hunter's particular needs . . . his needs alone, forgetting the artificial needs of the field trialer.

For example: doesn't it seem rather strange that American retriever-training books hardly ever suggest using the dogs as upland hunters? Yet of all the retrieving breeds, only the Chesapeake was originally used as a water dog. The Lab and the Golden, which by far outnumber the Chessie, were originally used as land retrievers and upland dogs, and it was not until they reached this country from England that their water skills were developed.

Because the field-trial game does not include flushing work, the subject of upland hunting has been almost completely ignored in training books. In like manner most books cover in great detail many things that are important in the field-trial game but a waste of time for the hunter.

THE OLD WIVES' TALE

As in many other areas of learning, many baseless old wives' tales have crept into retriever lore and through sheer repetition have soon become generally accepted as "fact." We shall look closely at these old misconceptions and try to see how they got established. Here is one example that has been proven wrong during the last twenty years. When I wrote *Water Dog*, I said that a hunting dog should live in the house with the family. This shocked the hunting fraternity, since they had always been told that it would ruin the dog's nose and he would be tougher if he lived alone in a kennel outside. That false piece of training philosophy must have been started by some old wife who hated her husband and his dogs. Now the scientific studies of dog behavior tell us that a better rapport between master and dog can be established, training can be made easier, and everyone will be happier, if the dog is treated as a full member of the family. Of course in some cases this might call for a slight readjustment . . . like a new wife. But what was said in *Water Dog* twenty years ago has now been proven true and is generally accepted by both the hunter and the field trialer.

Back then the field-trial game was dominated by the professional trainer. He ran a business of training his clients' dogs and running them in field trials. Many of the wealthy families had their own full-time trainers. The sport was practiced much the same as horse racing: wealthy owners came out and watched their dogs run in the event. But the owners didn't really "own" their dogs, the trainers did. They were the masters. Of course a trainer could not have sixteen or twenty dogs living in his house, so out of necessity they lived in a kennel. Even my wife would agree with that. Slowly, over the past twenty years, the sport has become more democratic, and the little guy has gotten into the act. He had one or two dogs; they were the family pets as well as his sporting dogs. This little guy could and did give his one or two dogs more training time than the professional could devote to each individual dog. Even more important, they lived together and a real bond developed between them. Today the amateur field trialer is beating the professional at his own game. Not only has the amateur learned to become a good handler, but he and his dog get real teamwork going. The record book shows that while living as a pet nothing has happened to the dog's nose, and as far as trials are concerned, the dogs are harder-going today, because the tests are more difficult. As for the hunters . . . ask any of them who have their dogs living as pets if their noses are affected.

The person who can build the necessary rapport with his dog will both win in trials and have a winner in the field. Today many of the top professionals will no longer train and run dogs for others in trials. They have switched their business to training you, the amateur, to train your dog and to run him in trials. Ask any field trialer whom he would rather run against in the last runoff of the day—an amateur with one dog or a professional who trains a whole string of dogs. I'll bet my dog's milk bones that he'll say the professional, because the amateur and his dog are a team that is hard to beat. So, once and for all time, let's bury the old lady who hated her husband and his dogs, and make our dogs house pets. (Incidentally, even the field-trial people have come up with some old wives' tales of their own. We'll look at some of these witches' brews later.)

THE HUNTER'S DOG

I wish I could make sure you knew what the job of the hunter's retriever entails. In training a dog, as we have said, you obviously must know what the final product should be, and you must also know the dog's potential. You just can't get a pup, take him hunting when he's big enough, and let him work only with the instincts his mommy and daddy gave him. Even the best breeding can't provide the control and performance you are going to need. Unfortunately, the standards that most hunters have for their retrievers are far below what the dogs could achieve. Here is an example: it's so typical it hurts . . . a dog is sitting on the floor of the duck blind. A pair of blacks circle to investigate the decoys. You and your buddy reach for the guns. You start the feeding call and crouch with your heads to the front of the blind. Old Knothead wakes up and senses the tension. The calling alerts him that the action is about to start. BANG . . . BANG! At the gun old Knothead starts his race, almost beating the gun. God forbid if anyone gets in his way. He

Retrievers have to be gentlemen, under complete control, and that is what we shall be after.

scrambles out of the blind . . . runs 10 yards to the water . . . flies 8 feet into the drink . . . swims 20 yards to the bird . . . is back in a flash to the shore, where he drops the bird so he can shake off the water. (Many a lightly hit bird has flown off from right under a dog's nose.) He picks up the bird and brings it to the blind, dropping it at his master's feet (another opportunity to fly off).

"How did you like that?" the master brags. "Fine," his buddy says. "Now can you send him for the bird I hit that went down about a hundred yards over in that marsh?"

No way could that dog get that bird, which he did not see fall. No matter how well bred his genes are, that kind of handling on a *blind retrieve* (a bird the dog did not see come down) can be learned only from you. A dog who will run out and retrieve only a bird that he sees, and that is it, has not yet earned the title of retriever.

There was a fine book written back in 1894 by a fellow named B. Waters. No one seems to know anything about Waters except that he must have been a man of means, since he paid to have his book printed himself. It's called *Fetch and Carry* and is the first book of its kind published in this country. Waters did a fine job, for his day, on the subject of training the hunting retriever. He analyzed both the dog and the hunter and told it like it was. I particularly like one thing he says: "The beginner is commonly satisfied with too low a standard of retrieving and his own standard of sport is not too high either. The educated retriever should have a perfect understanding of his handler, be obedient and know how to properly perform his work." That sure is a nice gentlemanly way of saying that most retrievers and their handlers are untrained nitwits . . . and unfortunately things haven't changed much in almost a hundred years.

My guess—and it is a charitable one—is that of every hundred dogs in the field about ten are worth their feed. It's really a shame, because the retrieving breeds are workaholics, have a strong desire to please, and because of these attributes are easy to train. The problem is that most hunting retrievers are used only a few weekends a year and the rest of the time live on unemployment compensation. That's not the dogs' fault and possibly not the hunters' either. A lot of the trouble comes from just not knowing. Try to explain a symphony to someone who has never heard classical music and see how far you get.

What we are going to do here is to start from the very beginning. We are going to show you that with a little direction you can have a hunting retriever before the dog is a year old. You are going to be the conductor of the concerto written for duck call and full orchestra, including a big reed section.

What is at the end of the line? ... This is it!

WHAT'S AT THE END OF THE LINE

I once had a chemistry professor who taught me an important lesson about learning something new . . . and it had a lot more to it than just chemistry. He walked in on the first day of organic chemistry and told us to put our books away. Then he started a lecture that was more like a magician's show. The only thing he said was, "This is what organic chemistry is all about." Then he went into a fanfare of experiments that was like the Fourth of July. The place sounded like a riot, smelled like a war, looked as if a disaster had hit, and had the beauty of a modern art gallery. He ended the lecture by saying, "You will be able to do all this by the end of the semester, but you are going to have to study some dry stuff along the way." He was right; it was dry, but I learned whenever trying something new to look to the "end of the semester" to see where I was going. If you know the end product you're after, know the direction to go in . . . with that perspective it's easier to solve problems along the way. Learning dog training is no different from learning chemistry.

What is at the end of the line for the retriever trainer? There are two areas to deal with. The first is control. We want a dog who absolutely responds to the SIT, STAY, and COME commands. You will be surprised at the exactness we shall demand on these basic commands. I shall say it now and you will be reminded of it many times: if you do not have these commands taught to a no-fault response you might as well not continue. *You must have them!* (Much more about this later.)

There are only three tasks that we shall require of the dog to play the hunter's game:

1. For upland work the dog will learn to quarter a field, working within gun range in front of the hunter just as a Springer works flushing game.

2. For the waterfowl hunter the dog will learn to do the toughest of single retrieves across all kinds of terrain and water obstacles. Such a retrieve, in which the dog sees where the bird is down, is called a *mark*. (You may be surprised later when we discuss double and triple retrieves to see how little additional training is needed.)

3. You must be able to "handle" the dog from your side by directing him with hand and whistle signals to the place of a fallen bird that the dog did not see come down . . . a *blind retrieve.*

I only wish there were some way you could see my ten-month-old pup performing each of these tasks . . . and his boundless enthusiasm for the work. Go along with me step by step and your dog will do the same.

THE THREE TASKS

A retriever will earn the title of a hunter when he can carry out three tasks: quarter a field, working like a Springer; retrieve waterfowl singles with dispatch (doubles and triples will come with experience); and handle to game he does not see fall. In the top picture, the dog must work within gun range . . . 15 yards. In the picture on the next page, he must have faith and believe in you. He knows that if he follows commands he will get his reward—the duck. On the right, we tried to get a picture of Tar retrieving a single. The birds came in before the photographer arrived. No more ducks came that day . . . that is hunting.

LET'S CLEAR THE AIR

Many hunters have the mistaken notion that field-trial stock produces dogs that are too high-strung . . . too "hot" for hunting. Over the years I've had hundreds of people tell me they want to get a pup, but do not want show stock because they aren't sure if show stuff has the necessary hunting instinct. They don't want field-trial dogs, they say, because they're too high-strung, but working, hunting stock.

I agree that show stock may or may not produce hunters. Too many of the show dogs have not been hunted for ten generations, especially the English show stock that is being sent to this country. Even the British hunters and field trialers do not use their own show stock for the field. But the business about field-trial dogs being high-strung is just another old wives' tale. I believe this notion comes from not understanding what one sees when he goes to watch a field trial. At a trial in America the dogs all wait in their crates in the cars or trucks until it is their turn to go into action. They know what the game is all about and they're literally like children who can't wait for their turn at playing. They hear all the commotion, with whistles blasting and guns booming and when at last they are released from their "jail," they know what is about to happen and couldn't be more excited.

Watch one of those same dogs after he has run and you will see the difference . . . from a maniac to a gentleman in one easy step.

The British handle their field-trial dogs differently. The dog walks with the handler all day on lead. He follows the whole trial and can be called into action at any point. There is no long confinement. Consequently he doesn't seem in the least excited or high-strung.

Another fact is that a field-trial dog's desire to retrieve is about as strong as his desire to eat. There is certainly nothing wrong with that . . . in fact, it's one of our main assets in training. Anyhow, what constitutes good hunting stock is not that well defined. Everyone seems to have his own idea of what a good hunting dog is and most of these conceptions are questionable.

There is one kennel that has used the same bloodline of dogs to accomplish three different jobs . . . in the show ring they won the national specialty championship, in field trials they produced a national champion, and their basic stock is being used to breed guiding dogs that lead the blind. This breeding has produced some of my own gun dogs.

The fact is that any smart hunter will seek out the field-trial stock for his gun dog. We'll be telling you where to find a pup to start and even how to pick the best pup out of the litter for your needs as a hunter.

We are going to begin with the pup and go through the training step by step. You will have to make sure step one is learned before you go to three. The basic commands must be learned firmly—we crawl before we walk, just as you can't learn spherical geometry without a firm knowledge of algebra.

Most hunters fall by the wayside in their dog training because they think it will take too much time and patience. Let me assure you that I am a man of little patience, and as for time, my travel schedule will match any traveling executive's. If you will go step by step, you'll discover that it will take only a few minutes a day when the pup is very young, and once you have the pup working for you, the field training will go faster than you think. I don't know any other way to say it than just believe, trust me. Read the whole book and see the direct, precise pattern of what we are doing . . . then believe.

This retriever-training book is not going to be a rehash of *Water Dog*. I am not just bringing that material up to date after its success of twenty years. This book will be complete in its own right. Its directions will be for the hunter only and that simplifies things. If you have a copy of *Water Dog* on your shelf, it might be a good idea to reread it. Some of that material will be covered here in a condensed version. It might be a good thing for you to refer back to it from time to time, but all the material necessary for the hunter will be here in this book.

The only thing that I ask of you, the hunter, is to believe what you read here. It is going to be made simple, and if I can do it, you can. If you are not going to believe, you might as well stop now and if you have not dirtied these first few pages you might still be able to get your money back.

If you still have the book, I want you to decide now to do the job right from the beginning. You are going to owe that much to your dog. Retrievers are such grand dogs that you and your family will have a love affair from the first day. You might as well fall in love with a worker.

WHERE I AM COMING FROM

There are a lot of books out there for you to choose from. I doubt that you have read any that I have not seen. Some have been around a long time and have been very popular. I am not exactly new to this field, but I think it's fair when a man sits down to write a book to give his readers an insight into where he is coming from.

Any of you who have read my columns in *Gun Dog* magazine know that I do not mince words. I tell it as I see it. I have nothing to sell . . . I do not train dogs professionally . . . I do not breed and sell dogs. In fact I am not a dog trainer in the usual sense of the word. If there is anything I have tried to do during these twenty years of dog writing it has been to be a dog thinker. I cannot take a statement on face value. That is how all of my writings have come about. *Water Dog*, for example, presented new ideas that drove the conventional dog trainers up the wall. It took years before they would even try them. It was the little guy, with his one dog, who made the book successful to the point that it now outsells all training books combined almost three to one. The same approach was used in researching the book on the history of the Labrador Retriever. I just could not take at face value what others had said before me, and found to my dismay that the dog writers of the nineteenth century knew more about dogs than they did about history. The first man to mention the Lab in the literature made a mistake, unknown to him, and everyone who followed just copied what he said until it was accepted as gospel. I spent two exciting years researching back through history to get the story straight and traveled 20,000 miles to check what I was discovering.

To watch a young pup develop is almost like seeing a miracle. To mold a dog, a very young brain, is a sort of creating . . . maybe not like a sculpture or a painting, but believe me, it is very rewarding. I honestly believe that I have the key to starting with a pup and making him into the working pal I desire.

I associate myself more closely with you, the hunter, than with the professional dog trainer. I feel I know you and what you want in a dog in the field better, because that was what I wanted when I started. I could not spend all my time with the dogs because I had other professions to follow, but that didn't make my desire for the dog any less. I had to find a way consistent with our life-style to accomplish the goal . . . a well-trained hunting retriever.

HOW WE ARE GOING TO REACH THE GOAL

There are two methods of training a dog. One is the natural method and the other is called the force system. But if we examine both systems of training we shall find that both require force . . . the difference between the two is in the degree of force.

Here is an example of that word *degree*: When a child of two takes a piece of candy, having been told not to, Mom sits the child in the corner to mull it over. I think that we can call this a natural-training method, but it

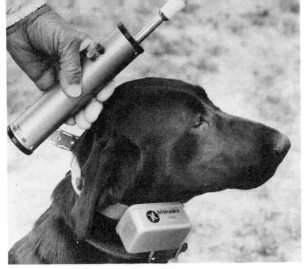

In the hands of an expert, the shock collar is a very humane way to train a retriever. In the hands of an amateur, it's disaster. In the force system, the whip can be used to prepare the dog for collar training. For the hunter, the force system is not the way to go. The natural method is easy and successful.

still involves a degree of force. Instead, if Mom merely says, "That's not nice," and lets it go at that, that kid is going to get into trouble later. At age ten, when he takes another kid's ball glove, he'll get a punch in the nose. We can say that represents the force-training method. The difference in degree of force—between sitting in the corner as a "pup" versus getting one's block knocked off later—is considerable. But there is force in nearly all constructive learning, and little or no force in negative learning . . . witness the mom who did nothing.

If, as we say, there is some force in all training and the only difference between the two systems is in the degree, then you will see that in our natural system the learning is going to be so gradual that excess force will not be needed . . . but firmness will. We shall not be like the mom who did nothing. Slingshots to sting a dog in the flank when he breaks on shot, shotguns at 60 yards to pepper a dog that won't stop on whistle, and even the electric collar are some of the force methods we shall not use. The first two methods just mentioned are barbaric; the electric collar is the most humane way of administering the force system. But—and that is an important *but*—the collar must be used by an expert or sure as all blazes the dog will be ruined. This is a pro's tool, and even some of them get bad results with it. In the hands of someone who knows his business, and if the dog has been properly introduced to it, the electric collar can produce wonders. As a quick fix in training it is usually disastrous.

The force retrieve, using the ear pinch to cause pain, is not needed to reinforce the retrieving instinct. In this method, when the dog opens his mouth to cry out, a dummy is shoved into it. Another system, with a string tied to two toes and pulled to create pain, is used by some pros. It will work, but a pro ruins many dogs before he learns how to do it. These systems are not for the hunter with his one dog.

A dog's learning is no different from a child's. I firmly believe that as far as the hunter is concerned, he does not need the force method if he goes about his training properly. Just as the child who had to sit in the corner learned his lesson, a young dog will learn his, too. Don't tell me your dog will SIT, STAY, and really knows those commands, except when he hears a gun go off . . . and then he breaks before he is released. That dog does not know his commands or believe you mean what you say.

The dog comes to us with a built-in desire to please . . . that is why we domesticated him aeons ago. Learning to learn is not built in . . . that is what you have to instill. The animal behaviorists have demonstrated that provided you start a pup learning at an early age he'll learn for the rest of his life. That gets rid of the old wives' tale that you can't teach an old dog new tricks. You can, as long as you start him learning when he is young.

The method we shall be using is the natural-training method. I feel that the average hunter, a guy like you and like me, can deal better with the natural method than with the force system. The collar may have become the field trialer's tool, but by no means do they all use it . . . with or without, they all can get remarkable results.

We shall show you a simple procedure, a gradual, step-by-step way to go. We shall start at the beginning.

Chapter 2

From Little Acorns Grow . . .

IN THE BEGINNING . . .

If Eve was fashioned into a fully formed woman from Adam's rib, as the account states, it was the only such event on record. Ever since then things have started as little acorns and into mighty oaks grown . . . and that includes puppies. Bending a sturdy limb is a vigorous job . . . bending a sapling is child's play. Similarly, training a grown dog is a tough job, but even a child can train a pup. We strongly advise the hunter to start with a pup, and that means one that has just been weaned. You are going to be surprised how fast things happen in that little ball of fur.

As a beginning trainer, if you start to train a dog who has not been living with you from puppyhood, you may have serious problems. If you have had the pup from the first and are starting training late, you might be able to do the job, but it will be harder on both of you and the results may not be as

From little acorns . . .   . . . mighty oaks grow.

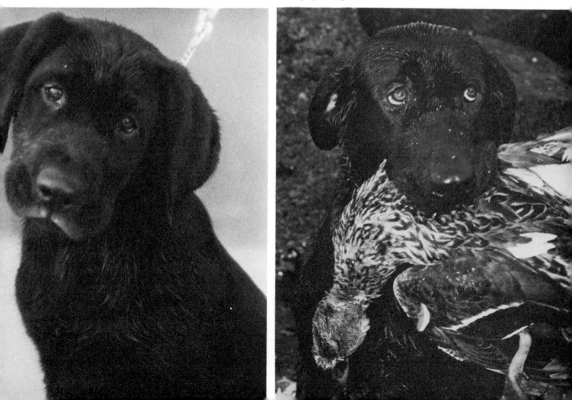

good as they could have been. As we go on, you will see what is considered to be too late. If that stage has been reached in your situation, you will have to take even a young dog back to "ground zero" and start with him as though he were a pup. Going back will require care on your part, because the young dog has already taken on some bad habits. You will have to follow the same step-by-step procedure as you would if the dog were younger. It is easier to accomplish the training when the dog has known no other way.

Since the old books on training were written, a lot of new knowledge has come down the pike. But over the years hunters have been traditionalists. We seem to like the old guns, the old stories . . . everything seemed better in the past. There is something nostalgic about our sport. New things go down hard with traditionalists. But I'm getting old enough now to know that it really wasn't that much different back then. "Ol' Daddy had the best dog you ever saw" you hear someone say. But back in the good old days B. Waters was writing about how bad the dogs were. Hunters tend to remember the good days and forget the dreary ones between. Ideas on how to train have been handed down from father to son or dog writer to dog writer ever since a chapter appeared some 480 years ago in one of the earliest books printed in the King's English. It is interesting to read the old writers to see how little ideas have changed with today's traditional dog writers. This despite the fact that animal behaviorists like Dr. J. Paul Scott and Dr. Michael Fox tell the new scientific stuff on learning in so easy a way, even my dog could understand it. But somehow the hunter seems to believe that that's not the way Daddy did it. In *Water Dog*, I spell out the new information in detail. That thinking, which is really not that new anymore, is extremely important to the hunter, and he's making his dog suffer if he ignores it. Here is that information again but boiled down so even your dog can read and comprehend it.

THE PECKING ORDER

We have enough problems, as a dog gets on into the serious training, without added ones that could be eliminated before they start . . . and it all starts at the very beginning, back in the litter. All animals that live in a "family" structure develop a thing the behaviorists call the pecking order. It starts as a competition for survival . . . a battle for food and warmth. The pup that learns to fight his way in to the bitch gets more food and will develop into a tough cookie. At the other end of the scale, the pup that gets trod on gets less food but survives by shying away to prevent the hurt. It is easy to understand that the first pup becomes the bull of the litter and the

other one becomes the wallflower. The rest of the pups will find their places in between. Don't think for one minute that these pups are not "imprinted" for life! They are.

It's important to take the pup from the litter just as soon as two things have taken place. First, the dog should be in the competitive situation with his littermates long enough to know he is a dog. Don't laugh. Pups who leave the litter at four weeks and live with people have a difficult time breeding later. Second, the pup should be strong enough to leave the litter. By the end of the seventh week both situations are covered. Then it is most important to remove the pup from his mates at that exact time. At this age, seven weeks or forty-nine days, the pup's mentality has developed to a point where he has already started to learn (see *Water Dog*, page 19). The animal behaviorists say a pup starts to learn and can be taught simple things unrelated to survival at five weeks of age. At seven weeks, when the pup is ready to go home, he is already learning and will continue to do so. That's when we want you in the act. He might as well learn the things you want to teach him, not what he'll learn from his mates. But there are even more important reasons!

YOU SHOULD KNOW . . . IT'S A MUST

I can't overstress the importance of understanding, before you pick a puppy and take it home, that a lot of your success depends on knowing and believing what the behaviorists have to say about dogs. When you take a seven-week-old puppy home, so much is going to happen so fast that if you don't know what it is all about and are not able to take advantage of the situation, you and your pup are going to have some struggle ahead.

We've poked fun at the old woman who hates her husband and his dogs and makes them live outside, and then there is a witches' brew from field trialers who believe that training should not start until a dog is six months or a year old. Some top-selling books still tell it that way. Tradition again . . . we got that idea from the nineteenth-century English writers. Then hunting dogs were trained by the gamekeepers who kept the kennels full of dogs. Their system worked well for them in their time. With a large kennel of dogs they had no choice but to let the litters grow and develop, then pick the dogs that showed the best promise and train them. With forty or fifty dogs, what system would you use? There is no reason to use that method if you have only one or two dogs, and since the nineteenth century we have discovered much about learning.

A young brain, be it a child's or a dog's, is like a sponge ready and willing to soak up all the information it can get. One question will prove my point. If you woke up tomorrow in Sweden, how long do you think it would take you to learn to speak the language—the vocabulary, the grammer, the idioms, the dialects—the works? If you lived to be a hundred you would still speak with an accent. I have a hard time understanding someone from Brooklyn, but a Swedish baby will get most of his language by the time he's out of diapers and ready for kindergarten. Are you going to believe it if I tell you that a nine-week-old pup will learn to obey the commands SIT, STAY, COME by voice or whistle . . . or both? Don't doubt it . . . it's being done every day. You are not reading wishful thinking. This has been demonstrated and proved by one of the most prestigious animal behavior laboratories in the country—Hamilton Station of the Roscoe B. Jackson Memorial Laboratory at Bar Harbor, Maine. This work was directed by social psychologist and Rhodes scholar Dr. J. Paul Scott, and this laboratory is where Dr. Michael Fox took his training. Their findings revolutionized dog training. The original work is not new . . . it has been around for twenty years.

This scientific work was initially done with guide dogs for the blind. The five critical periods of a pup's mental development are spelled out in Appendix II. They have completely changed when we start training a pup.

Here is the proof of the pudding of what you are about to read: the dogs that lead the blind are now trained with this early-training method. Before this system was used and dogs were not started on their training until they were physically big enough to lead the blind, only 20 percent of the best-bred litters were able to take that most rigorous training. Now, using the early-training method, 90 percent of the dogs of that same breeding become guide dogs. How can dog writers today ignore this information?

Here are some more absolute musts for the hunter. The scientists do not tell us to take the dog out of the litter *about* the seventh week. They spell it out to the exact day, the forty-ninth day of life. Their reasons for this are, first, they want to stop the effects of the pecking order before they have had time to mark the dog for life; and second, this is the best time for you to become the mother substitute. A third reason—and vitally important to the hunter—is that a dog will make a bond with man during the period between the seventh and twelfth weeks, and never again in his life will he establish as strong a rapport with a human as he does during that short period. Twelve weeks sounds very young, but by then the dog's brain has been physically formed to its adult size . . . the only thing added will be experience. Read that sentence again; it's a shocker.

SOCIALIZATION IS THE KEY TO LEARNING

Socialization will be the key to the dog's development. A pup that has no human contact, but lives only with the litter for its first twelve weeks, cannot be trained to be more than a companion. If the litter lives isolated for the first sixteen weeks, the pup can accept no training from man.

Here are some of the things that Dr. Michael Fox has to say: "What socialization does is to make the dog attach to you so that it will become more trainable. If socialization is delayed, say until three or four months or even older as happens in some kennels, the dog will not be sufficiently bonded to you to make him readily trainable."

About socialization, Fox also has this to say. "We often see two distinct types of poor socialization. In the first, the dog is afraid of people. In the second, the dog is less afraid of people, but is afraid of everything else, and this type reacts to correction with submissiveness rather than obedience. No pressure can be put on them in training." This is why it is so important to get that pup out of the kennel and home with you, so that you can immediately start giving him all kinds of experiences. The pup travels in the car . . . meets people . . . hears the noises of the town . . . even goes to the gun club to hear the big booms. Fox calls this *environment enrichment*, and it should take place between the fifth and tenth week. After the tenth week a pup in unfamiliar surroundings will show fear. A pup kept in a pen too long gets what Dr. Fox calls "kennelosis."

Dr. Fox states that the eighth week is a very sensitive period in the pup's life. His advice is to lay off and avoid being severe with the puppy during this week, so the pup does not develop an exaggerated fear reaction to the stress of minor mishaps, surprises, or attempts at training. The real secret, according to Fox, is to give the pup a sense of control and mastery over his environment by giving him a chance to explore and learn. If he is kept kenneled during this period he does not develop a sense of confidence. This negative imprint of being afraid of new experiences is going to get in the way of learning. And if the pup's environment is not enriched by the twelfth week he will show serious impairment.

Take note, "old wives," Dr. Fox finally comes up with the answer to those who believe that a dog's place is in a kennel outside. He says that it is important to avoid threatening or stressful experiences during the eighth week and to give the pup good social and environmental enrichment during those early weeks. These things are essential to the dog's later well-being, but dogs do not keep like pickles in a jar on a shelf. Well-socialized dogs, if allowed to vegetate in kennel runs between bird seasons, can actually regress through boredom, depression, lack of social interaction . . . and their motivation is sapped.

Dr. Fox says another interesting thing: if you have properly socialized the dog to people and things, just after weaning, and between twelve and sixteen weeks of age the pup still shows signs of fearing strangers, you probably have a dog that will give you training problems.

Putting what Fox and Scott have to say into practice is as easy as falling off a log. When you take the pup home at seven weeks you become the mother to the pup, and you will find that the eighth week is just a fun time for all. The pup learns the big new kennel and immediately trusts everything. No pressure is put on him. Once the pup is over this important fun period—actually the very next week, the ninth—the first simple commands will be learned. I have never seen this fail . . . a nine-week-old easily learns his ABCs . . . SIT, STAY, COME. Have you known retrievers who would not pick up a bird? That doesn't happen if a dog is given a bird to play with, to smell, to try to retrieve at the age of ten weeks. When this is done there is no fear or hesitation later.

There is a story that comes down to us through literature about a king, in something like the fourteenth century, who wanted to find out if Hebrew was really God's chosen language. The experiment he ran was to place infants in a home where they had no human contact, except for basic needs,

Give 'em love, horseplay ... get 'em socialized.

and never heard the spoken word. The king wanted to see what language the children would speak on their own. The experiment failed, however, because without love and socialization the children died.

So these early weeks in a puppy's life are critical to his success in future training. During these weeks a young dog passes through five distinct periods of learning. These periods, at which we shall look more closely a little later on, are over by the time the pup is 112 days old, or only sixteen weeks of age. So there is no time to waste. If you see what can be done with a young pup, you become a believer. If you try this early training—and we shall take you through it step by step—then I'll bet my dog's best bone that you will believe.

THE BIG MISCONCEPTION

There is something about man that I can't explain, but have found to be true. A person seems to believe the first story he hears. If someone comes along later and tells a different version, the listener tends to disbelieve. It is obvious that the scientific information on the dog's mental development is rather new as compared to the much longer history of dog-training literature. One belief that has been "on the books" a long time seems to be another of the baseless old myths, but it is a rather ingenious one. You perhaps learned it as a child, and I'll bet you don't even know when you first heard it. It goes like this: there is an age ratio of one to seven between man and dog. A one-year-old dog is like a seven-year-old boy, a two-year-old dog like a fourteen-year-old teen-ager, a three-year-old like a twenty-one-year-old man, a seven-year-old dog like a guy over the hill, and a nine-year-old like me with one foot in the grave. The error in this thinking is that the ratios concern physical age . . . not mental. If you wait until a dog is nearly a year old before training him, because that is the equivalent of the age at which we send our kids to school, you are going to have a lot of unlearning to do.

Today we can teach children to solve arithmetic problems almost as soon as they can talk. Now don't tell me that Uncle Harry says that you will ruin a dog by starting him too soon . . . even if Uncle Harry does field-trial his dogs. You teach a pup to be housebroken as soon as he moves into your home. That is for your convenience. Why shouldn't he be taught some other things at this age for his own good . . . and in the long run for yours?

The name of the game in training a dog is to teach him to learn to learn. Most dogs come into a family and live on social security from day go, and they never work a day in their lives. A dog that learns to learn will go on learning the rest of his life. It all starts the moment he recognizes his name. Teach a dog and a bond will develop between you . . . teach him at seven to twelve weeks of age when the dog establishes the strongest bond with you and you will have a team operation started.

Can you give me a logical reason why most people will train a dog to be housebroken immediately but refuse to go on and teach him anything else? They can't understand why at six months old, when his ways are set, good old Knothead learns only when it is time to eat . . . and how to get around them by being a jolly fellow and doing only the things he likes, when he likes. Obey commands? Sure, if it suits him at the moment. A pup has to learn to learn early or he'll become a spoiled brat . . . a pest instead of a pet.

Chapter 3

Choosing a Pup

THE PROBLEMS

So much has been written on this subject that I flinch when it comes my turn to discuss picking a puppy. I don't intend just to rehash the same old material. Some of the standard information will have to be covered for the fellow who has not read it before, but if you don't get some new information out of this chapter, I'll let you kick my neighbor's dog.

The problem that most hunters have is finding a pup of good stock when they want one. Up until 1984 the hunter using retrievers had no national organization to turn to as the field trialer had. For forty years the field trialer has had a publication that followed his activities, but now the hunter has his magazine. It's called *NAHRA News* and is the magazine of the North American Hunting Retriever Association. The hunter is usually not as mobile in his activity as the trialer, so he has not known what is going on in the puppy market. Trialers got to know each other from coast to coast . . . hunters hardly know the guys in the next county. The NAHRA publication and activities have changed all that. A NAHRA studbook gives the hunter important breeding information.

There is nothing like seeing the parents of a litter work. Obviously, if the dogs on both sides of the pup's lineage are proven workers, the material is there. We parents know that that is no guarantee of getting a good worker. Some of our kids can come from the best "stock" and still get messed up, but it's usually either the fault of the parents or there is too much unfortunate influence from the kid's peers. We shall try to eliminate both of these causes in the raising of your pup, by teaching you to be a trainer as well as a parent and by controlling the dog's environment. Then he'll learn only what we want to teach him.

Where are you going to get a pup when you want one if your cronies don't have good working-stock pups at that time? Unless you have inside information, stay away from the newspaper ads that list pups for sale—AKC papers and all—throw the paper away! Unfortunately we're developing two separate lines of retrievers both in this country and in England . . . and the English are taking the lead in this. Most of the dogs today are from show stock, and the English have had too much to say, through the show ring, about the Lab in this country. The Lab is the third most popular dog in Great Britain, and most English retrievers have not been hunted for ten generations. Hunting in England is not a democratic sport as it is in this country; the average person or dog does not have the opportunity to hunt. Even worse, the English show judges don't even know how we hunt here or what we need in our hunting dogs . . . and yet they are judging our dogs! They don't even seem to know what is needed by hunters in their own country, since, as we have already said, the British field trialer and hunter (who play their sport differently than we do) do not use the British show stock in the field. The show people here and abroad play their own game; they're doing their act—breeding for the show ring. Ask any person really interested in the ring and he will agree that if British judges are invited to this country to judge a show, the entry list will be doubled. Somehow it's felt that the judges bring a touch of the Queen with them. That makes for a good take at the gate for the show club but disaster for our dogs. Naturally the judges will place dogs that fit what they know, see at home, like, and breed themselves. If you want to win in the ring you have to get that British look in your dog, and the way to do it is to have the English judges/breeders ship over to this country dogs of their "style." I don't think that is too honest, but then again I stay away from the show business. Put one of those show retrievers on the Eastern Shore in a tough goose blind and you will kill the dog. I can hear the show people screaming at me on reading this, and some of them would have a perfect right to do so, because there are plenty of them out there who are honestly trying to keep the "work" in the dogs. The problem is that it is hard to know which show breeders are really doing a good job and which ones only talk a good game. Of course, if 90 percent of the hunters themselves don't seem to know what a good retriever is, or what the working retriever's potential should be, how can you expect the nonhunting breeders to know? I've argued this for years and gotten lip service as answers. With NAHRA in existence no more talk is needed. Hunting stock is now easy to evaluate.

All puppies look pretty much the same but what they've "got" will show up only later when it is too late and the whole family has fallen in love with the wonderful critter. If you are going to want a hunter, you might as well get all the odds on your side by buying working stock.

WORKING CERTIFICATES

When the newspaper ad includes a line stating that the sire, bitch, or both have working papers . . . burn the paper! Those working certificates, from the tests I've seen, aren't worth the paper they're written on. To the unsuspecting hunter, such an ad looks enticing—working papers—just what he is after! Burn the paper, but keep the funnies. Working papers are supposed to prove that the hunting instinct is there. This is not the platform to argue that point. . . . My responsibility is to hunters. Buy stock that works and hunts—not the instinct.

Pedigrees of dogs are not easy to understand. There are some geneticists who consider a pedigree to be a mathematical shell game. Parents give each pup 50 percent, grandparents 25 percent, great-grandparents 12.5 percent, great-great-grandparents 6.25 percent, until it gets to the point that a fine dog in the background gives three strands of hair on the tail. They can also draw you a "shell game" diagram that will show that a pup can get as much from the grandparent as from a parent. It's all made too simple. When the eggs of the female meet the sperm of the male, there are 2 to the 100,000th power either/or decisions that are made. The only way the average hunter can deal with this is to select a pup with as much working stock behind it as possible, and take his chances . . . he can't be a god. Try to be at least a saint . . . make sure both parents of the pup have what it takes. David Follansbee, an important Brittany Spaniel breeder, wrote, "There is an old Spanish saying, 'Brave cows produce brave bulls.'" We in this country seem to consider the sire more important in a breeding. Dog people in Europe feel the female is more important. I do not know who is right so I go for both!

What are we looking for in the pedigree? The titles will give you a good clue. The MHR (Master Hunting Retriever) signifies that the dog has proved his ability as a hunter. Dogs who have won points toward the title prove that they have good basic hunting ability. These points are a real working certificate. Field-trial titles are: FC (Field Champion), AFC (Amateur Field Champion), CFC (Canadian Field Champion), or the top distinctions of all, NAFC (National Amateur Field Champion) and NFC (National Field Champion). CH (Champion) designates show champion. DUAL means the dog has won in the show ring and is also a field champion, and there are not many of them around.

How do you read these papers? Obviously the more champions in the pedigree, the better. The closer they are to the direct line to the pup, the better. Master Hunting Retreivers or Field Champions as parents are better than a National Field Champion as a great-grandfather. Tar, the pup whose story is told in this book, has a fine pedigree. Of the sixty-two names listed in his background there are thirty-two Field Champions, seventeen of whom have both FC and AFC titles; there are three DUAL champions, and five National Champions, two of whom have both NFC and NAFC titles. His parents are an FC and an FC plus AFC. His grandparents include two FC plus AFCs, one NFC plus NAFC, and one bitch for a grandmother who didn't make the grade. We all seem to have one black sheep in the family. It is interesting to see that the champions are dispersed almost equally in his ancestry, seventeen on the bitch side, fifteen on the sire. That is a hot pedigree. I don't understand genetics, so I want as much on my side as possible. If Tar got a little from here or a lot from there, I want those littles or lots to be hunting ability, not just pretty hairs on his tail.

WHERE TO LOOK FOR THE PUP

NAHRA News can be obtained by becoming a member of NAHRA, for $25.00 a year (NAHRA, P.O. Box 1590, Stafford, VA 22554 (tel.) 1-800-421-4026). The *Retriever Field Trial News* is a newspaper put out by the two national field-trial clubs in this country (4213 S. Howell Avenue, Milwaukee, WI 53207).

If you have a line on a breeder, ask for references and check them out . . . I've yet to hear a huckster hollering, "Rotten apples for sale".

What about pet stores? *Forget them!*

Another good source is a NAHRA club or field-trial club that also holds NAHRA tests in your area. If you do not know who or where, write to the American Kennel Club at 51 Madison Avenue, New York, NY 10010, and ask for a listing of retriever clubs in your vicinity. *NAHRA News* carries such a list. Call the local club secretary and find out when a trial, field test, or training session is to be held. Go out and talk to the people at the event, see

Some of the pups will be rather self-assured.

what they know about pups that are available. See the dogs work so you will get to know what you are after. Get acquainted with the people . . . they'd rather talk dogs than tell sexy jokes.

BOY OR GIRL PUP . . . WHICH?

It's not dealer's choice when we get our kids . . . we takes what we gets. But when a pup is about to adorn the rugs we can choose male or female. As far as hunting ability is concerned, they both have it. I know of only one type of hunter who might have an advantage with a male and that is the goose hunter. Males are usually bigger and stronger and can handle a big bird with greater ease. Other than for the goose hunter, the gals do just as good a job— as we fellows are finding out these days. Some feel the female is easier to train and better around the house . . . they are stay-at-homes. The males grow to be better-looking dogs (take note, you gals), and I've always found them just as affectionate as the females. The one disadvantage of the female is her two periods of heat each year. You can have that problem for as much as forty days a year. It's rough when the bitch comes in season the same day as the ducks. We can't do much about the birds, but the bitch's heat period can be postponed, though with possible side effects or messing up her cycle. If you plan to get a bitch, talk to your vet about the new sprays and other methods. After all, I sell books, not prescriptions.

LET'S GET THE PUP

Getting a pup is a hit-or-miss proposition with most people, and this is the first mistake along the way to getting a good hunter, as you will see in this chapter. Some folks buy a pup as they would a pair of pants from a mail-order house. They see it for the first time when they pick it up at the airport. That is OK if you have a breeder who really knows his business and is honest with you.

What are you going to pay for the pup? When you buy pants, the cost is the only investment you are going to have. If the cloth is good and they are well tailored, they are going to cost more. It is not that way when buying a pup. The original cost is the least part of your investment over the next twelve or so years, so you might as well go for quality.

All the books give the usual things to look for. Do the pup's teeth have a matching bite? . . . Are the teeth white, without brown stain? . . . Is the skin supple? . . . Is the navel OK and not popped out? . . . Are the ears, eyes, and nose clear? These things are all fine, but you should make sure that the sale terms include your vet's looking at the pup. He is the one to make sure about all the physical problems. A good breeder will give you a record of the shots the pup has had. The pup should come with early protection against distemper, leptospirosis, and parvo. Conscientious breeders will be able to tell you the history, if any, of hip displasia and PRA, a serious, blinding eye disease, in the parents. Registration papers usually follow in the mail.

There is an old hunter's method of picking the best pup from the litter. Put your hand in the barrel, pick one up, turn it over to see if it has the plumbing you are looking for. If not, try again. That method is just about as good as the system most people use.

People like to go through the ritual of playing with a litter because they feel that at least they are doing something to help in making the choice. The prospective buyer sits in the middle of the litter and plays with all the pups. The one that pulls at his cuff, pounces through the pack, climbs up into his lap, and paws at his shirt to give him a love lick is usually the one that wins his heart and gets bed and board for life. Unfortunately, after the system of buying a dog by mail order, this method of choosing could be your biggest error. By taking the pup that shoves his way through the crowd to give you that face lick, most likely you have picked the dominant dog in the litter, the bullheaded one . . . the toughest to train.

THE ANIMAL BEHAVIORISTS CAN HELP

Scientifically we now know a lot about a litter of puppies. In the last chapter we referred to the five critical periods of the dog's mental development. We shall spell the details out further here because we are going to have to know them. There is more about this in my book *Water Dog*.

The *first critical period* is from day zero to day twenty-one. A pup during this time is like a house that is completely built, with all the furniture in place and appliances ready to go; the only thing lacking is the electricity to run things. The pup can be taught nothing during this period except very simple things having to do with survival. The scientists say that on the twenty-first day, in all breeds of dogs, the "electricity" is connected.

The *second critical period* is from day twenty-one to day twenty-eight. At this time the senses start to function. It's a traumatic time for the pup, for actually it is a shock to the system. Mother is an absolute must for the puppy at this time.

The *third critical period* is from day twenty-eight to day forty-nine. This is the time when the pup will start to explore and learn. This is when the pecking order begins to be noticeable and by the end of the period it's well formed. This is the period we shall be most interested in for this discussion, because at the end, at the seventh week we shall pick the pup and take him home.

The *fourth critical period* is from day forty-nine to day eighty-four. We shall talk about this period later in more detail. This is when socialization and environment enrichment should take place. The pup will go to kindergarten during these few weeks to learn his early commands . . . SIT, STAY, COME.

The *fifth critical period* is from day eighty-four to day one hundred twelve. Starting with the twelfth week the puppy will go to real "school." At the end of this period the pup will become a typical adolescent and will want to do things his own way. This lasts for about a week. It is best during this time to lay off the training until the pup gets his sense back. If only it were that easy with our kids!

It is during the third period that we shall be selecting our dog. We know that there are pups in the litter with potentially different personalities . . .

that is what the pecking order does to the litter. Now we have to find out which pup is which.

We shall be using a modified version of the Campbell procedure, a Puppy Behavior Test*, to try to find out where individual pups stand in their litter's pecking order. We shall explain why the change in the test is being recommended and show how we shall use the modified version.

The purpose of the testing? We recognize that all litters develop their own pecking order . . . from the dominant pup to the submissive one, and all the ones in between. For our purpose the individual personalities, such as the dominant and the shy, have to be identified. As you will see, the first step in selecting will be to eliminate these two at the extremes of the pecking order. By the seventh week the pattern of the order is established.

But before taking up this procedure in detail, I should note that it cannot be expected to work in every case. Other methods of pup evaluation have also been devised, though the best of them may be too technical for the average hunter. Recent information has modified the views of many scientists and breeders about puppy testing.

Because I am not a breeder, I have to listen to what the breeders are saying. Many have spoken to me, but Jack Jagoda of Southland Kennels in Stafford, Virginia, has expressed it best, so I will let him be their spokesman.

"I object," says Jagoda, "to the buyer coming into my kennel armed with a copy of the Campbell Puppy Behavior Test (which seems to be the most popular puppy-selecting method at the moment) and asking my permission to run it. I have deliberately run the test at different times of the day and have gotten different readings on the same pups. It seemed to have a lot to do with the mood of the pups at that time. My observation is that it can't be done in an afternoon. You have to get the whole picture to make this kind of a decision, and a one-shot test is not going to be accurate, especially when given by people who buy one pup every ten years." Jack and his wife, Diana, use a practical testing system. He says, "We've got our method: we devote many hours of personal contact each day to our pups. We know where each one stands. If the buyer wants to know, we can tell him."

There is another serious problem with this test that has been brought to my attention. Breeders tell me it does not seem to work well in litters of certain breeds, such as the Labrador and the Golden. The pups are very

*The original Campbell procedure was developed by William E. Campbell and appears in his book *Behavior Problems in Dogs* (American Veterinary Publications Inc., Drawer KK, Santa Barbara, California 93102).

often socially extremely uniform . . . so much so that testing for pecking order can be very inconclusive. Michael W. Fox, one of our leading animal behaviorists, when asked about this agrees that a test such as the Campbell procedure may work well for the terriers or the German shepherd, but is not as good in breeds that when full-grown are all mild-tempered and just natural "baby sitters." Fox approaches the selection problem entirely differently. In his book *The Dog: Its Domestication and Behavior* is a chapter titled, "Heart Rate and Plasma Cortisol as Predictors of Temperament." This is a very technical discussion of the relation between heart rate and temperament. Pups with the highest resting heart rate in the litter seem to be more outgoing, inquisitive, and independent and this continues into maturity. Scientists like Fox are not seeking a "cure-all" test for picking puppies. There is no such thing, according to them. What they seek is a battery of neurological and physiological tests that will reveal the personality pattern of a pup. I just don't see a hunter picking out his pup with a stethoscope.

The truth of the matter is that the buyer of a pup is at a disadvantage. The breeders are the ones who could have all the answers if only they took the time and had the knowledge and desire to study their pups closely enough to give the customer the guidance and information he deserves. In some ways buying a pup is like choosing a wife through a marriage broker— there has to be trust someplace.

So far what we have been talking about is a way to identify the aggressive, outgoing, timid, dependent, or passive aspects of the pup; these are all socially oriented qualities. But there is more to the selection of the hunting pup than these social attributes. How do you test for the hunting attributes of a dog? Jagoda marks the Lab litters with a spot of different-colored paint, males on the neck and females on the rump. As they grow week by week, he can keep tabs on what "color" is doing what. He gets to learn which one attacks the food vigorously and which one shies back, how they respond to play and to him. This simple observation gives a quick overview of the social order. When it comes time, at the fifth week, to judge their hunting skills, a wing-tied pigeon is used to get the pups used to the bird. It's even put in the pen with the pups and they all live together. At seven weeks a wing-clipped bird is used. That's real excitement. The bird is flown on a lawn. The aggressive hunters, who are very much desired, will chase and retrieve on the first introduction. Just how the pack chases after a bird shows the ones that "have it." You may see all kinds of reactions, from the bold retriever to the pup who wants nothing to do with that "thing."

Where does all that leave the hunter?

Dr. Fox seems to feel that simple tests give the buyer "something to do" and make him feel he is having an input into the decision. I feel that the Campbell test has merit, but that the procedure can be made more practical with some modification. The animal behaviorists say the test looks good on paper but has its limitations and should not be considered as gospel. But for the average hunter it just may be the best tool we have.

There are two main objectives when picking a pup out of the litter. One is to eliminate the bull of the litter, the dominant dog, the one who thinks he's going to be the boss, and in like manner eliminate the shy wallflower, the one who will be so submissive that it will turn over on its back and give up any time it is reprimanded. The other objective is get a pup you like . . . a pup that shows a rapport with you. Look at it this way: there is no need for a little old lady to buy a Ferrari. Same goes for the hunter. He's going to be better off with a dog that will be easy to train, not bull-headed and not as high in "horsepower" as the dog the field trialer would want. The field-trial dog will have to take a lot of training pressure to obtain the precision required. The bull of the litter has a better chance of not folding under the pressure of the electric collar and the exactness required; he'll have an inner reserve with which to "fight back." The average hunter won't be using a stringent force-training method, so he won't need a dog who can stand up to that kind of pressure. This does not mean that the hunter's dog won't be an aggressive hunter; it means that psychologically he won't be as difficult to handle. It also does not mean that the dominant dog is the only one who will make field-trial material . . . it just means that the trialer has the odds on his side if he takes the dominant dog.

The hunter will make out best if he takes a pup out of the litter who is in the "middle of the road"—and that is what we shall try to show with this modified Campbell test. The hunter will want a dog who has get-up-and-go but not "charge," a pup who is spunky and not a sissy. We'll steer away from the "wallflower" in the litter, who can be even more of a problem to the hunter than the bull of the litter.

We can go on the assumption that if the pup is a bull at five weeks, he'll most likely be a bull at five years; if he's people-oriented at five weeks, there is a good chance of his being people-oriented at five years; if he's shy and unsure at five weeks, he'll probably be the same at five years. Of course there is no guarantee, and that is the weakness Fox finds with the Campbell test. A dog can be seriously "scarred" or helped in his rearing.

Jack Volhard in his book *Training Your Dog: The Step by Step Manual* uses and expands on the Campbell procedure, but for the show people, not the hunter. Rutherford and Neil, in their book, *How to Raise a Puppy You Can Live With*, again spell out the Campbell test. I too have used this test. It worked for me and it's the only "ball game in town" for the average guy.

A MODIFIED VERSION OF CAMPBELL'S BEHAVIOR TEST FOR PUPPIES

The test should be run before the litter is seven weeks of age. Each pup should be carried individually to the test area, which should be unfamiliar to the puppy and have nothing to divert his attention. A fenced-in lawn is best. When you take the pup to the test area, say nothing. Just gently carry him in your arms. The carrying should be without incident; we do not want the pup to be upset or excited. There are four parts to the test. You are trying to find the most aggressive and most passive pups as they compare to one another. With Labs and Goldens, don't be surprised if you find out that they test similarly. Run the tests during the time of day when the litter is alert and playful.

Does He Like People?

When you reach the middle of the testing area, set the pup on the ground. Then quickly walk on until you're about ten feet from the pup. Kneel down, get the pup's attention by clapping your hands and gently coax him by voice. You are to observe how quickly and willingly he runs over to join you.

He ran off! He's not people-oriented. On the next page see how his littermate did.

You will be comparing each of the pups, noting whether his tail is wagging or drooping. Is he lively, or hesitant, or does he simply not respond to your invitation? This test indicates the extent to which the pup is attracted to people, or whether he is a shy "loner," and how much self-confidence he has.

This friendlier pup hesitated, then came with a little trepidation, but enjoyed it.

Come with Me

Stand close to the pup and then walk off in a casual fashion. As you do so, carefully observe the pup's reaction. How willingly and enthusiastically did he tag along after you? Was his tail up, and was he underfoot? Did he charge you, bite your cuffs, and challenge your progress? Did he follow hesitantly with his tail down, or did he simply refuse to follow you?

This pup stayed where he was put down. The tester waited. The pup decided he wanted no part of this . . . this shy dog wanted to hide. . . . not a good pup to take.

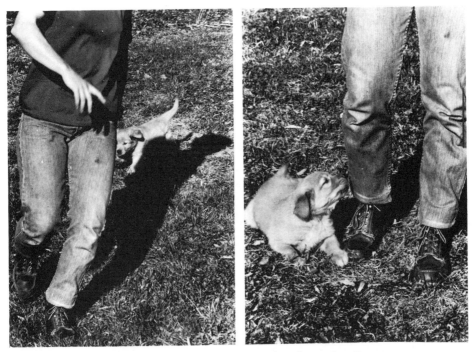

The next pup, rambunctious, brash, tagged along with no hesitation. He was . . .

. . . aggressive, chewed trouser cuffs, interfered, and took the role of the leader. This pup will need a strong hand in training.

Lying back and making no effort to resist shows he could be shy . . .

Learning Takes Restrictions

Turn the pup over, without being rough, so that he is lying on his back, and with your hand on his chest hold him there until he reacts. Observe his reaction. Does he squirm and fight back, nip at your hand, or growl? Does he resist at first, then give up and settle down? Does he try to lick your hand or does he make no resistance at all? Is he a little bull or a lamb? By the degree to which the pup either resists this treatment or goes along with it, you can judge what his reaction to physical control or discipline will be.

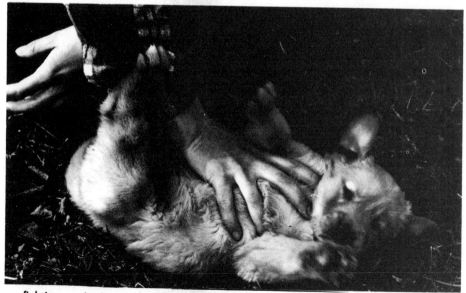

. . . fighting, squirming, and struggling show he's headstrong.

This pup couldn't have cared less and he accepted the person as the boss.

This one fought. We're looking for a pup that's middle of the road in temperament.

Who Is Going to Be the Boss?

Lift the pup with your palms under his tummy. Hold him with his paws three or four inches off the ground until he reacts. There is little the pup can do. He's either going to accept it or not; in this situation you are the boss. How does he react? Does he struggle, and if so, how vigorously? Does he try to lick your hand, or do nothing? His resistance or lack of it in this situation indicates the extent to which he is willing to recognize you as the boss.

HERE IS WHAT IT ALL ADDS UP TO

To put it all into the simplest terms, we want to eliminate the pups at the extreme ends of the pecking order. The hunter will do best with the "middle" dogs. That's the best dog for the average hunter. He'll be hardy enough to take the training, will socialize easily, and will be an all-around good choice. The bull will be too aggressive. The passive pup would fold under stress and be too submissive.

The two tests, "Does He Like People?" and "Come with Me," will be good indicators of how easily the pup will socialize with people. The "Learning Takes Restrictions" and "Who Is Going to Be the Boss?" tests will be good indicators of how the pup will take to training.

How should the hunter go about using all this information? I would suggest that he visit the litter and spend as much time as possible watching the pups eat, sleep, play, and then run the test procedure outlined above. After eliminating from the choice what he considers to be the most aggressive and most passive pups, take the remainder, one at a time, off into a field and evaluate how they each play "fetch" with the wing-clipped pigeon. And then there is a personal factor that has to work into all this. After all, you are not buying a few pounds of hamburger. One of those pups, while playing retrieve, will "win you over." It may be his style, the excitement the pigeon arouses in him, his desire to bring the bird to hand, and his looks—all these factors may figure in.

The next thing the hunter has to consider in all of this is his own personality. If he is a tough, demanding trainer, he should go for the more outgoing pup. If he is in the middle of the road, the dog should be the same—but if he is a shy guy, he should still not take a shy dog. You have to fit yourself into this test to make a good decision.

If you don't believe the test, try it anyway—what do you have to lose? And that is just the point. It can help to spot the dominant and shy dogs . . . any one of the others could make it fine into a hunting marsh.

I guess you already know that socially dogs are not much different from people. I once had a great-uncle Louie who should have been tested. There is usually one scrapper in every litter, and I guess that goes for your family, too.

Chapter 4

Getting the Training Started

ANALYZING THE HUNTING PROBLEMS

Whether you are a duck hunter or an upland hunter, the dog has to do what you want, not what his instinct tells him he wants. Let me try to analyze the hunting problems and break them all down to their simplest common denominator, so you will understand the dog's job.

As a flushing dog, doing upland hunting, the retriever will be expected to work just like a Springer Spaniel. He will quarter and comb the fields and woods, but the bottom line is that he must work within gun range. Flushing a bird 100 yards out may be fun for him but not for you and your cronies. The dog's mommy and daddy gave him his fine nose and the instinct to hunt, but you have to teach him control, to hunt where you want him to do it. Keeping the dog in shotgun range depends on his obeying the command COME! If you allow a young dog to range only so far and constantly bring him back within shotgun range, he'll finally learn that that is the distance you want. It's simple; COME is the key. Show me a dog who has to be put on a check-cord to hunt in range and I'll show you a dog who does not obey the command COME!

Breeding produced the desire to hunt. Control . . . quartering, working close, have to be taught.

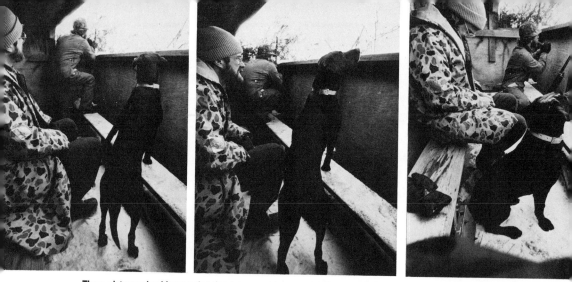

These pictures should prove that dog learns on his own what the game is that we play. I could not have taught him this. Jet alerted us that the birds were coming. He saw them first, followed their flight, and when the caller turned them, he knew what was happening. On command he, too, took cover. This series of pictures was never finished. I stood up and shot the gun. . . . Jet retrieved.

For the duck hunter, we are going to add some manners to the training. In the blind the dog is going to have to sit and stay. That's not only for the comfort of the hunters but also important for the dog's work. The knucklehead who rips through the gunners at the first shot to get out and get that bird is unsafe—and a running dog will not be able to mark a fall well, or while he is running he won't even see that a second bird is hit. The dog must sit, stay, and go only on command when the action is over. He must learn to sit at heel; that's where he learns the command. But as you will see, he must also learn to sit on command at any distance from you—20 feet or 200 yards. This will be the base from which we shall teach the dog to handle, to follow your hand and whistle directional signals. Handling starts with command SIT and we shall build from that later.

What we are trying to do here is to give you an idea of what is at the end of the first semester of "chemistry." Before we get started on the actual training you must realize how important the SIT, STAY, COME commands are going to be. I do not mean so the dog just knows the commands . . . I mean so the dog will do them—*right now!* Don't be frightened by that. We shall start so early that this will become part of the dog's life. At ten weeks, on leash he'll be doing SIT, STAY, COME by voice or whistle. If you have never seen a retriever handle, you should get to a field trial and see how magnificent they are. You will be impressed. Much more on this later, but at this juncture you must recognize how precisely these commands must be executed as the training progresses. Teaching the basic commands should start immediately. As you will see, the pup can do it. It will be a big time-saver to get this early training established well. Doing it later is possible, but it is easier to bend a sapling than a tree.

BRINGING A PUPPY HOME

The puppy comes home to the new big kennel when he is seven weeks old. In actuality, training starts immediately. Just having him in your home sets the stage for learning. For the next five weeks we'll be in the fourth critical period and the pup will learn at astonishing speed. The pup starts in preschool before kindergarten. The teacher's first role with preschool kids is to take the place of mother. You will do the same with the pup. Part of his training is to learn that it is you who is giving him a secure place to live, a warm bed in the kitchen, good food three times a day, and lots of playtime when he's awake. You'll play fetch with him with a sock stuffed with rags and it's going to be a romp and just fun. The pup will soon learn that no matter what the rest of the world thinks, the boss is a nice guy.

It'll only take a few days for the pup to settle in. Watch him learn. He'll know where the water is, where his food pan is kept. The rattle of the puppy-meal box will bring him alive. Tar, the pup I am now training, learned to go up and down the steps to the outside on the first try and by the second day was doing it on the run. That was fast. You'll see that he has a great desire to be with you except when he naps. From the beginning we keep a Kennel-Aire in the kitchen. That is his private place. No one is allowed to disturb him when he goes into it. That is his "castle," and that makes him feel very secure . . . the kennel is never used as punishment. We also have a Kennel-Aire in the station wagon. It is like the castle in the house, so we transfer that good place in the kitchen to the car. Tar traveled 1,000 miles before he was ten weeks old. As a hunter he's going to have to travel a lot . . . why shouldn't he learn it now? Dr. Fox calls that environmental enrichment.

By the end of the first week Tar had learned many things. One was that he was not allowed to chew on the wooden furniture legs. My wife would go around smearing hot Tabasco sauce on the wood. Although the house smelled like a great big shrimp cocktail, our pup got the "taste" and I guess he didn't like shrimp. Actually we always had a knotted rope chewy ready as a substitute. It is such fun to watch pups discover things. I never before had seen a pup that took an interest and watched TV. Tar did from the start and even seemed to like my programs. Look, this part of the training is easy, but

Never discourage a pup from carrying anything in his mouth. If he has the wrong thing, praise him while taking it away and immediately give him the right thing . . . a dummy. We had a friend whose wife screamed at his pup every time pup got his mouth into trouble. His dog upped and quit one day. A few years later . . . so did he. Isn't there a moral here somewhere?

important—you're the mom: his development and your future success can be made or broken right here. This is the time when the pup will form his strongest bond to human beings . . . and without you at this time he would never reach his full potential.

All this means plenty of love, attention, play, and care, but your role as teacher must also not be neglected. A dog lover can only love his dog; a dog trainer can love and train. Right from the beginning—only a few days after the pup arrives—training starts. We want this little critter to learn to learn; to do that, he's got to start forming the habit early, before he learns that most other dogs get what he gets without any learning or work.

The dog's first job is to become a good member of the family. In my book *Family Dog* I show how to bring a pup on fast for his job in the home. We shan't cover that material here. I'm sure you all agree that housebreaking should be taught immediately. Remember, don't be too severe on the pup. There is no earthly reason why the same thinking should not be applied to SIT, STAY, COME.

TEACHING THE WHISTLE COMMANDS

In the next chapter we shall go into more detail about how you communicate with your dog so he will know what you want . . . and there is a lot more to it than the vocal commands. In this preschool training it is all going to be done as fun and games, so we'll mostly hold off until the dog "goes to school." But there is one part of "talking" to your pup that you will start to teach in this early period.

Some twenty-five years ago I was hunting on the Eastern Shore with some friends and we were in two separate blinds about 60 yards apart. The day was cold and windy, perfect goose-hunting weather. But as usual the geese were flying miles away from us. It was bitter, and I decided that as we had no action I would find out if the fellows in the other blind had any "milkshakes" with them . . . strictly for warmth. I stood up and cupped my frozen hands and shouted over the gale that was blowing to get their attention, "JACK! . . . HEY, JACK! . . . *Jack!*" I got no response. I shouted for all I was worth. I figured that one of two things was happening: either they had milkshakes and had finished them so they were oblivious to everything, or they just could not hear me. I blew one blast on the whistle to find out which it was . . . up popped three heads. I can't remember whether they had anything to warm the innards or not, but that little scene got me thinking. If on such a day we had had geese, and there were blind retrieves involved, how in blazes could I expect a swimming dog, 100 yards or so out in the water . . . in that surf . . . in that wind . . . to hear me hollering commands at the top of my voice? No way. I decided that I would try teaching a dog to do all his commands on whistle. That would make the job easier for the dog, and I would start teaching him that language from the beginning. After all, a dog does not understand language as such. Dogs can be trained to the few words they must know in any language, be it English, Russian, French, Chinese, or Yiddish . . . so why not Whistle?

Here is the whistle system:
    One blast means SIT.
    Two blasts mean MOVE.
    Trilling (beep, beep, beep, beep) means COME.

For the moment that is enough about the system. We shall cover a lot more about it later. The reason I bring this up here is that we shall start with that whistle language right away with the pup. We shall teach him all the commands with the voice and with the whistle also, so that he will respond to either. I do practically all my talking to the dog in the field with the whistle. I start this right away. After all, if you want a Swedish baby to learn his language not long after he is out of diapers, you do not wait.

TAR'S STORY . . . MINUTE BY MINUTE

Here is exactly, almost to the day, what you can expect from that little "sponge" that wants so much to please and play with you.

Tar was brought home on the forty-ninth day. He traveled 500 miles without as much as a whimper in his Kennel-Aire in the station wagon. He met Jet, almost five years old, for the first time as they traveled side by side in their crates. Once home the pup took over. At the first meal he decided grown-up food was better than his mush, so he tried to get into Jet's dish. Jet "scolded" him, and never again did the pup try that act.

A visit to the vet was one of the first things on his itinerary. He came off with flying colors. As soon as the vet said he could go out into society, Tar was given every opportunity. He was taken to the drugstore . . . to the library

"Is this what Dr. Michael Fox calls environmental enrichment?"

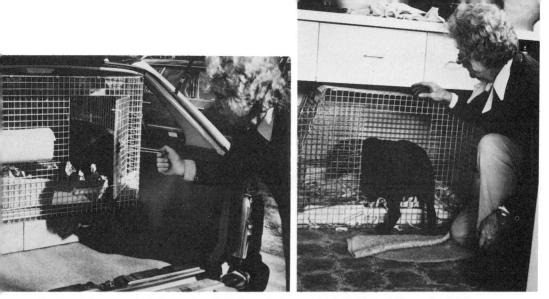

The Kennel-Aire is a pup's kitchen castle, and there's one in the car so he feels at home while traveling. It'll become his first-class plane accommodations; his home away from home while hunting.

Tar received every experience I could think of that would be valuable to him later. From the woods to the cleaner's, he met all kinds of things and people. We even went to the library, thinking we both might learn something. We learned that dogs with kennelosis are afraid of their own shadow.

The first taste of gunpowder. Dogs are not born gun-shy; man makes them that way. The big boom will never frighten a pup if he hears it from the cradle. Tar was brought up to the gun slowly, yard by yard.

(under my coat) . . . to the post office by car. He met and played with everyone he saw. He stood by as I watched road construction going on. In other words, he was put into the environment of everything I could think of that he would run into during his life. No way was he going to show any fears of anything. At home he had all the people attention he needed to be socialized. He had me right there to feed him and play so we could make our bond strong. Jet got into the act and took him on as a new brother around the house. He let the pup chew on him from sunup to sleepy time. Tar was surely environment-enriched—not only to the things around him but to all he was going to see in the field. We took walks into the woods. He went to the gun club and heard the big noise and even smelled and tried to carry the crazy-colored birds.

LIFE IS NOT A BOWL OF CHERRIES

"Life Is Just a Bowl of Cherries" is a song title that most of you will not remember . . . that gives you some idea how old I am, and the song too. Even if Tar sings it at the top of his voice he's got to learn what the words mean. While living in the kitchen, until he was housebroken, Tar quickly learned not to bark and bite the ankles of the lady who was doing the cooking. If he didn't stop he was put on a leash and tied to a doorknob until he learned just to hum the song . . . barking and screaming did him no good.

'Oh, what a cruel world. I want to bite that nice lady's ankles." Tar has to learn right from the start that he does not always get his way. He is no different from any child who wants all the attention. He has to learn now not to become a spoiled brat. It is almost the first lesson in his training—it sets the stage.

He had to learn from the beginning that we don't always get our way. A pup is no different from an infant who wants all the attention all the time. A baby will cry when it is hot, cold, wet, hungry, bored, and soon learns it can get attention by crying. Sooner or later Mother will start to teach the child that crying will not get him things that he does not need or that are not good for him. A spoiled child is a pain in the neck to deal with, and a spoiled dog is no different. Command NO is the first one pup hears, and you must make sure that he learns that you mean business.

A dog and a child come into this world with one thing in common. They both think that everything is for me . . . me . . . me . . . me. Mother's job over the years is to teach the children they have to live in a world with a lot of other me . . . me . . . me's. That is called growing up—learning moral values. The pup has to learn the same thing, but because a dog has no moral sense he has to learn what he can and cannot do by rote. You cannot explain to a dog that begging is not allowed at the table. You have to show him by never letting it happen. But if one person slips, the dog will learn that maybe someone will slip again. To be a good trainer you have to be consistent in your training, and everyone the dog deals with in the home has to abide by that rule. The point is that when you decide to give a command, it must be obeyed at ten weeks or ten years—the only difference will be in the method. Dogs must learn that commands are to be followed, not considered.

"OK boss, I'm ready to learn!"

FETCH . . . THE NAME OF THE GAME

Tar was very lucky . . . the lady who made all those wonderful smells in the kitchen loved to play fetch with him just as much as his master did. We played the game with puppy dummies just as much as we could. Without even knowing it, Tar became crazy to play fetch. We'd try to get the pup all excited by being excited ourselves. We'd encourage him to bring it back, but there were no rules—just throw the dummy across the room and let him chase, grab, run around with it, and have a good ol' time. When he would bring it to us, almost by mistake, he would be praised and the dummy would immediately be thrown again. He soon got the idea himself that if he brought it back the game continued. Nondelivery is a problem that so many young dogs seem to have. They believe, I think, that the dummy is theirs and by bringing it back to you they have to give it up and lose it. That's why we threw the dummy immediately when Tar brought it all the way back to hand. Starting a puppy this young, I have never had the problem of a dog bringing the bird halfway, then stopping to consider whether he should come all the way, or the problem of having to chase a pup. The first duck that Tar delivered, when he was about the same length as the bird, he delivered out of the water and up a 40-foot sloping bank to hand. He did not even drop it to shake. Tar learned to deliver at such an early age that he has never, *never* failed to deliver a dummy or a bird directly to me.

The first thing, of course, is to develop that desire to fetch, but the way you do it will pay off in dividends later. First, get all excited yourself, and jump around teasing him by swinging the dummy in circles around his muzzle. Get him to want it, oh so badly! When he is excited, toss it a few yards. Then, as we said, as soon as you get the dummy from the pup, shake it to renew his excitement again and quickly throw it again. It is the chase he likes. Never hold the dummy too long between throws. You want to get the idea across to him that if he brings the dummy back to you the game will be continued. If he gets to believe the dummy is his, he will not want to give it up, but will want to play chase. That will become a more serious problem when he is a little older. He is going to have to learn to deliver to hand, so start him young and the trick is to get that dummy out of your hands as quickly as possible. Just as soon as you see he does not need the swinging of the dummy around his nose to create the excitement, stop it and simply keep throwing the dummy for him to retrieve. But don't stop the excitement on your part. Keep up a chatter of encouragement, with fun in your voice.

Our retrievers come with the instinct to carry things in their mouth.

FETCH . . . MAKE 'EM LOVE IT!

Three things happen as soon as the pup comes home. First, he's given a warm, friendly home with plenty to eat. Second, as soon as he knows his name he will be taught his early commands. Third, and very important, is the "fun fetch" game. It's easy and starts immediately. A puppy dummy is all that is needed. The pup's mommy and daddy gave him the retrieving instinct, but it's up to you to develop it. As far as hunting is concerned, you will never have to force-train a retriever if you play this game often enough. How much? You will get tired before he does. Remember, keep the dummy moving. Don't hold on to it, or he may get the idea it's your toy and just run off with it to make it his. He's learning that if he brings it back, as the bottom picture shows, I'll throw it again. I'm hoping he learns that's what I want, so I don't have to go chasing him to get the dummy later on. To start (left picture) we both get excited. The throw is shown at the right. I use a "trill in" call on the whistle just to get him used to it. He doesn't know yet what that means, but it won't hurt, will it?

Some may have it more than others, but no matter what you get, you have to develop it. I hated to try to answer the question I was asked just yesterday on the phone: "How can I get my dog to pick up the bird and bring it to me?" The dog was eighteen months old and, from what I was told, loved to hunt upland. The dog would find and flush game like a trooper but wouldn't retrieve. When I asked when he was taught to fetch, I was told that it was when the pup was about nine months old. The only thing I could suggest was for the person to take the dog all the way back to the beginning and play fetch just as if he were a pup—get the dog excited about the game and see what happened. The caller said the dog did not like dummies. I answered that there was only one other answer that I could see, and that would be to force-train him to fetch. When I explained how to go about it, I had the sinking feeling that, for the amateur trainer, there went another dog down the drain. It is just so unnecessary. Get the pups started early . . . get them to love the game.

All pups may not be as easy to train to bring the dummy all the way to hand as Tar was. If the dog stops on his way back and looks at you, saying, "Come get it. It's mine!" run away from the pup and call his name as you run. Clap your hands and get all excited. As he runs toward you, turn in your tracks, swing around, and take the dummy from him. Give the pup a lot of praise; show him that that is what you want.

For the pup that drops the dummy and then ignores it, you have to show him that that is not what you want. Play with the pup by swinging the dummy all around his head. You have to get excited about this game—jump around while you are doing this. Get him excited too, and when he really wants it badly, toss it a yard or so. When he picks it up command HOLD. Repeat the command. If he refuses to get the idea, on the command HOLD put your hand around his muzzle and hold the dummy in his mouth. Keep repeating the HOLD command. Go slowly with this; he'll get the idea.

There is an interesting story that retriever people should know. Do you have any idea how the U.S. Customs Department trains dogs to sniff out drugs in packages? They will do it with any good-size dog but like to use Labradors. The dog is taught to play fetch with a rolled-up towel. The towel is taped to keep it in a roll. They play the game for hours, for days, until the dog would rather play than eat. When the dog brings them the towel they then have a tug-of-war and get him even more excited. The next step is to throw the dummy into the woods and make the dog use his nose to find it. He'll come bounding back with the towel for his game of tug. Then they

Tar is happy now, he's crazy about the dummy.

I've seen eight-month-old dogs getting a bird for the first time and being scared half to death. Get a pup on birds early. He may think you are giving him dinner and want to eat it. Let him play with it; it'll pay off in dividends later. Tar tried to pick his bird up, but it weighed almost as much as he did.

1. Ten weeks old and getting his first live pigeon. He is teased with it and it's thrown a few yards.

3. Excitedly, he's called back, and back he comes delivering to hand. Fun for all!

cover the dummy with a sleeve that has the same smell as the drugs, but from a harmless chemical. The dog learns to sniff out the simulated drug. (The dog never comes in contact with the real thing—they are not drug addicts, as some have reported.) When he brings the towel back with the sleeve on it, the handler slips the cover off and plays tug, often lifting the dog off the ground. They have a great old time. When the dog is wild about the game, he is ready to go to work for them. He is taken near packages at airports and post offices. If he smells his favorite aroma, he'll literally tear a package or the interior of a car apart, if allowed to, to get to his "dummy" so he can play fetch. The handler, who carries the rolled towel in his belt, throws it at the dog's feet when he finds that right smell and gets excited. The dog, chewing

2. He bounds out, picks it up with no fear. He even seems proud.

and digging, using his teeth and paws, stops when he sees his dummy. He has his reward and the officers have the drugs . . . and the address on the package.

There are two things that are absolute musts during this preschool period. The desire to play fetch must be developed; get the pup just as crazy about the game as the sniffing dogs are . . . but don't ever play tug-of-war with him. That will develop hardmouth, a real no-no. Use only dummies—no balls or sticks. This is all taught during playtime.

The other must is starting the commands SIT, STAY, COME, and they too are learned as play lessons.

START THE COMMANDS SIT, STAY, COME

Teaching your dog the three commands SIT, STAY, COME begins with the dog's name. When the pup comes into the house he is given his name immediately, and the name is used every time he is addressed. This becomes important.

Here is the way it worked with Tar, and it was almost like magic. We watched his response to his name. For the first week or so the name was just one more gibberish sound from the big people in the house. I would test him to see if he knew his name by calling him when he was busy doing something like chewing a bone or an old glove. With his back to me when I called his name he paid no attention until he was nine weeks old, to the day. That evening he was frolicking with Jet in the middle of the living room. I called his name: "Tar!" He stopped and looked at me, then went back to tormenting his "big brother." My wife looked over to me and said, "That's it, he knows his name." The pup had graduated with honors from preschool and the next morning started kindergarten.

KINDERGARTEN . . . A RETRIEVER'S FIRST STEP

Tar was right on schedule. Every pup I've worked with, or those I've heard about, have shown that name recognition comes within a few days of reaching the age of nine weeks. That's the signal . . . that is the time the pup is ready to learn his first school lessons.

Here is the exact way it happened in Tar's young life.

It was late, that night when Tar was sixty-four days old, when I was convinced he recognized his name. Before breakfast the next morning we went to work. I put a thin leash on him, which he had been used to from our strolls in town, and walked him a few steps at my side. I commanded SIT, held his head up high with the leash, and with my other hand pushed his rear end down. One word was used, firmly: SIT. Then I walked him a few more steps and repeated the command and helped him understand it by plunking his rear end to the floor and holding his head up at the same time. We did this just six times . . . then we all had breakfast.

Command SIT. Lift the head and push down the bottom . . . hold up the head and keep repeating SIT.

Switch the leash to the left hand. Move in front of him. Show him the hand signal. Step back . . .

. . . The hand signal will hold him as you slowly move back. All motions should be slow, or he will break to be with you. When you get to the end of the leash, drop down to his level and call COME. He'll want to be with you and will come. Use the voice command and the whistle. He'll learn both.

At noon we did it all again . . . only six times. I had to plunk the rear end on the first attempt, and only had to touch his rear, to remind him what SIT meant, on a couple of the other tries. At supper time we did it six more times. The plunking was over and he only had to be reminded once with a touch of the finger what he was to do when he heard SIT. At bedtime, with the leash in place, he sat on voice command six times as we walked around the living room, and it only required holding up his head and a sharp, firm command SIT. He was doing fine.

Next morning before breakfast I added the whistle. I commanded SIT and immediately blew one short, staccato blast on the whistle. He remembered the voice command and put his little behind on the rug. He only needed help with the touch of a finger once. School was over after six SITS by voice and whistle. Before lunch we were back in class for six more tries with both the voice and the whistle. He had it. "By God, I think she's got it!" sings Professor Higgins when Eliza Doolittle sings "The Rain in Spain." And I was just as thrilled by My Fair Dog! At dinnertime I used only the whistle. He did it six times. That night we had a ball around the house. With leash on, Tar would sit on either voice or whistle. The fun was to watch the little fellow respond. He didn't just sit . . . he dropped his rear end like a hammer. He was cute. He wagged his tail and you could see he was enjoying the fun.

When we tried him off leash the success was about 50 percent. He'd back up, wag his tail, and bark at me. You could see he knew what I wanted but was not sure if he wanted to do it. Back on the leash he was his old hammer self.

In total time spent teaching this, I'm sure it wasn't an hour . . . and so many hunters say they just don't have the time to train a dog.

Of this much I was sure, Tar understood the command SIT by whistle or voice. It would be a matter of practice to make him firm. When he was in a new situation or there was a distraction, he had to be helped. When Dick Hay, my neighbor, came over to retrieve a tool I'd borrowed, I bragged about what the pup could do. I put on the leash, blew the whistle to show Dick, but all the pup wanted to do was play. Our success was nil. Dick's comment: "That's a dumb dog."

Within two days, however, six times at a session, Tar had the command down pat on or off leash. The proof of the pudding came at pudding time. Older dog Jet, on hearing supper being prepared, would go into a fit of joy. Puppy learned that one fast. They jumped and barked . . . this was their time! They were being saved from starvation. They screamed, "Oh, what a

No matter how important the food was, Tar sat on whistle. A good test to see if he understands.

wonderful person you are to prevent cachexia and malnutrition." When they both reached a crescendo, one blast on the whistle had both rear ends on the deck and the propellors were wagging in neutral. In all the excitement of the upcoming feast, Tar had responded to the command. Now it was a matter of training sessions and springing the command on him when he least expected it. Outside in the front yard the game was easier to play. While running or cavorting, the whistle brought him to a sliding halt. It was a fun thing to see him respond . . . he'd be in some crazy position, legs askew and at the same time trying to get his rear down.

Believe me, there is no magic to this. There is nothing special about Tar—any pup can do this! Everyone who sees the little bundle of fur respond thinks it's cute. Cute nothing . . . this kid is in class. You just have to realize the pup wants to learn, will learn and can—it is just a matter of believing it and trying it. This is strictly play games; no force or reprimand is used or needed.

STAY . . . KEEP SITTING ON IT

STAY is a must command for the duck hunter in the blind or boat. Eventually the SIT command will include STAY; they become one but they are taught separately. This is the command the British hone to perfection. Their dogs will move their heads and wag their tails as scores of birds are flown overhead and shot. The idiot who breaks on shot thinks we climb out of a warm bed at 4:00 A.M., go out in the freezing weather, get wet putting out the decoys, chilled waiting for the flight . . . solely to play a game for his benefit.

STAY is an easy command to teach. It goes with the SIT command like hand in glove. In fact a hand, with or without a glove, is how it is taught. Tar learned what the word *stay* meant in a day or two; it is that simple.

After the command SIT is given and being obeyed, step from the side of the pup to a position in front of him. Extend your left hand, and reach out, holding the leash so it is straight up over the pup's head. Keep a little pressure to hold his head up. With the right hand show the pup the universally understood hand signal for "stop," the palm of the hand toward the dog—just as the traffic cop does. Put it right in front of the pup's nose and command STAY! Keep repeating the command softly. If he starts to get up, quickly command STAY a little more firmly and lean over and push his rear end down. On the second try you will see that you can take a step backward, letting out a foot or so of the leash as you go. By the end of the day you will be at the end of the leash. Don't expect him to hold SIT for more than a few seconds at first. By the end of the third day he will hold it half a minute or more with only an occasional reminder to STAY. There is no whistle command for STAY. Later one blast of the whistle will mean SIT and then,

Food is the test, not the means of teaching. Show him his dinner. Step back, command STAY.

automatically, also mean STAY, until the next whistle command tells him to move.

In two or three days you can do this with the pup off the leash. If he starts to get up and move . . . start over. Later, after you are sure he knows the command, you can spring at him if he goes to move and quickly command SIT, STAY! For now, these are only play lessons. Two or three lessons a day is all it will take.

Leave the leash on and drop it on the ground. Walk backward, holding the hand in the traffic cop position. You will be able to get across the yard and he'll hold . . . try it and see for yourself.

For the retriever, this command has to be executed in rather exciting situations. But no matter how tempting the stimuli, the dog must remain at stay. I saw an incident at the National Championships in England that showed discipline. A bird was shot and fell a yard in front of a dog and lay there flapping, flopping, and kicking . . . the dog never budged until the judge walked over and told the handler to have the dog pick it up. That impressed me. When I got home I took Jet to a tower shoot. A bird was shot dead, hit the snow and slid between his front legs, and lodged under his body . . . he never moved. He looked up to me and waited for me to hit the whistle twice.

Once the pup has the command off leash I test him at mealtime . . . make him work for his supper and see if he really understands the command. I'll give him the command, then walk backward to the other side of the yard and make him sit and wait until he is released to come running to eat. In a week the traffic cop signal can be eliminated and the voice command will do the whole thing.

I called Tar with the whistle. As he came, I blasted once. He stopped, sat, so he got his food.

COME . . . WHETHER YOU ARE HUNTING WATERFOWL OR UPLAND

COME means just what it says: Come toward me . . . right now! SIT, STAY will be your controls; COME will be your first moving command. A dog that is not under control at heel is worse when he's out free from you. I've seen both duck and upland hunters almost have a stroke trying to get their knotheads back to them. Working under the excitement of game causes such a dog to "do it on his own." If the dog does not learn the basic commands at home, at your side, how do you expect him to obey them in the field when he's 100 yards away?

It is almost an inborn instinct for a pup to want to come to you It is the easiest of the three commands to teach. At this preschool age we are not going to force anything. We are going to rely on the fun he has being close to you and use that in teaching the command COME. A little later we'll want him to obey no matter how good the bird smells are, or if he has his own ideas about where he wants to be. If "Old Citation" goes running around in the backstretch racing to win a photo finish with a pheasant and busting birds all the way . . . you're going to be hunting alone.

How do we teach a pup to understand the command COME? Once the pup will sit and stay, and you have stepped back as far as you can holding the 6-foot leash, you are ready to command him to COME. As you step backward, you will be standing . . . the hand is outstretched with the traffic cop's signal to stay. Then drop down on your knees or haunches and command COME. The pup, who wants to be close to you, will come automatically. You can start from the beginning using both the voice and the trill whistle for this command. If the pup is reluctant to come, you can gently pull him in with the leash as you give the command. If this is necessary, be sure to use lots of praise. In a day or so, forget the voice, and he'll do it on the trill whistle. At twelve weeks he will do it off leash—no problem! If he learns it at this age, why wouldn't you expect him to do it at a distance later?

At a field trial when Tar was only twelve weeks old, I met a hunter who saw the pup go through his whistle training as he was being fed his lunch. We were back at the cars waiting our turn to run the big dog in a Gun Dog Stake. The pup was just there to get one more experience in his young life. This fellow came over and said, "I have a young pup and he'll do that too. It is amazing how young they learn, but I learned that the hard way. I had a two-year-old that I thought was a sensational hunter. If I dropped a bird he got it and that was all I wanted. He wasn't well trained but he did the job.

"I lived in Florida and we did a lot of jump shooting on the edge of the river. I bumped two and dropped one. As fast as the bird hit the water, Jock hit it too. He was fast. As he was halfway to the flopping bird I saw an alligator slither into the river from the opposite bank. I shouted and whistled frantically for Jock to come back. He charged on for the bird . . . gave one yip and disappeared. This time I'm starting my pup early and *really* training him!"

That's not a usual hunting story unless you're training alligators, but I saw just as tragic an incident on the Eastern Shore. In the blind next to mine there was one of those dogs that seemed to think his master spent $1,000 to dress like an Eskimo, paid $1,000 for his gun, $1,000 for the rig, and $1,000 to hunt this marshy point, just so he could swim to retrieve a duck. It was all for him. So when guns went off and a Broadbill came down in the swift current beyond the point, old Knothead charged out and hit the water. The Broadbill, who was more stunned than dead, saw Knothead coming and swam and paddled for open water. Seeing the upcoming danger, the hunter whistled for all he was worth. When the bird hit the main current, with dog in pursuit, I lost sight of both in my binoculars. . . . Neither returned.

The stories do not have to be that tragic to prove a point. An out-of-control dog is a pain to have around. If more than one dog is working, and only one is not under control, he'll ruin things not only for the other dogs but the hunters as well.

HOW FAR ALONG ARE WE?

Let's look back and see how far we have come. The pup is only twelve weeks old. The animal behaviorists tell us that we are at the end of the period when the dog establishes the strongest possible bond to his master. In these short five weeks you began as the dog's mother and ended as his friend and master. Your role as teacher has been set. You have two main purposes for the dog: to be a good citizen in the family, and to become a hunter. The pup understands the three basic commands and is on his way to becoming a retrievaholic.

Allow this period to pass without the early education and you'll be doing the dog and yourself a disservice . . . and you may have one strike against success. We are not implying that all can't be done later—it can, but you might need a two-by-four to get the same things accomplished that we have done with only play games. And . . . without the early fetch games the dog may not have the driving enthusiasm to retrieve.

Any kind of training can be accomplished by the force method by a competent trainer. Field trialers like the force method because it makes the dog faultless, like a machine run by a computer. It is great to see, but the hunter need not spend that kind of time, energy, or money to come up with a dog trained by the natural method that will really do his job.

In this natural method early training is an absolute must. Is there a stronger way to say that? You should see by now that SIT, STAY, COME is going to be the name of the game and you are well on the way toward establishing it. Let this time slip by with a dog that has a strong desire to retrieve, and his desire will override obeying what you want him to do. Let this time slip by with a dog that does not have a strong desire to retrieve, and he may never develop that drive.

Training a very young pup, before he learns what he can get away with, not only teaches him the commands themselves but also that he must do what you want, when you want it done. If nothing more were accomplished during this time when the dog is learning to learn, you will still be way ahead of the game.

Life has some restrictions for all of us . . . why should it be any different for a dog? I don't believe that young pups or children left to their own devices will only do good. They'll become self-serving. They are not born with a moral sense, which children can learn but dogs can't. A dog must learn by rote what is correct and incorrect behavior. . . . You can't reason with him. By repetition and more repetition a dog learns what is acceptable. If an animal can learn from the beginning, doesn't it make sense to start as soon as possible? Tar was not exceptional . . . more like average. Any pup will learn his simple commands by the age of twelve weeks with about ten minutes of teaching and five minutes of repetition each day.

I took Tar to the Gun Club outing when he was twelve weeks old. It was not very fair, but the ladies made more of a fuss over him than me. They wanted to hug him and cuddle him when I took him out of the station wagon for lunch. Of course Tar and I went through our SIT, STAY, COME routine before he was given the food. The ladies could not believe what they were seeing. Two of the women thought it was wrong that he should have to work for his food and were sure that at this age he was being ruined. One woman agreed with what I was doing and said that I had a special talent for training . . . baloney! . . . I have no magic wand. Anyone can do it, if he tries—anyone! You've just got to believe it can be done, and try it. You'll find that it's simple.

The sequence says it all. Tar is not much more than a ball of fur, yet he knows what I want . . .

. . . He comes on the trill whistle and stops on the one blast. The hand reinforces the whistle . . .

. . . Try teaching all this later and you will have a small battle. Tar's pattern is set for life.

A lot of love goes with all this early training.

Chapter 5

Making 'Em into Workers

THE BELL RINGS . . . REAL SCHOOL STARTS

Tar is now twelve weeks old. His brain has reached its full adult size. Now we have to put the lessons into it by repetition and by gradually making them more difficult. We have really set the stage for all this in the play lessons that went before. The only difference is that now we will *make* the pup do what we want. It is all very simple; we continue what we were doing before, but now we do it with a commanding tone of voice and whistle and handle the pup in a positive way. Of course there is still no real reprimanding. You will be starting this period with the pup only twelve weeks old and it will end when he is twenty weeks. The commanding tone and positive handling will be gradually introduced as you see him develop and as he learns to understand you and what you want.

A commanding tone of voice is just what it says it is . . . *it means business if necessary.* From this time on you no longer request the dog to do what you want, you *demand* it. Commands can include the dog's name and then one word: "Tar, SIT!" The name, if needed, is for attention; the one-word command conveys what he should do. A commanding voice is not a shout, but it's firm. There will be plenty of time later for shouting . . . you will want to hold that in reserve. Do not put a lot of extra words into a command. Don't say, "Come on, boy, come over here and sit down." A dog does not understand language as such, but he does get the one word by rote and he "reads" the tone. You can do all the sweet talk during playtime. The tone of voice tells him it is playtime—not the words. There are two tones: for play and for business.

We shall start to use what we talked about earlier: Without language, dogs come to depend on their own "reading" of us. We humans can lie to each other; dogs can't. But you can walk toward a dog without saying a word and he will know if you are angry or pleased. They read our stance, our movements, and expression. They can even smell trouble. They develop this sixth sense much further than we do; they have to in order to live with us. To be a good handler you must learn to give commands. Then you must make sure the dog does what you say, because he is quick to sense that you don't mean it if there is no follow-through. Tell a dog to sit, and if you do not make him do it he'll learn fast that you are all talk and no action.

Handling the pup in a positive way is as close as you should come to a reprimand at this tender age. In preschool, when you taught STAY and he broke and came to you before he was called, you started all over by giving him a pat and showing him what you wanted . . . first SIT, then STAY. Now if he breaks from the sitting position you take hold of the collar and take him back to the place where he was sitting and firmly command SIT . . . STAY . . . or blow the whistle one blast and show him the traffic cop sign for STAY. He already knows the commands, so it's now a matter of demonstrating that you *want* it done. Don't be rough—that will come later too—but be firm.

These are just two simple examples of voice and handling to show how to play the role of teacher. The problem most beginners have is that they know how to play friend and mother, but they don't know how to change their hat to play teacher. Then they wonder why their dogs need a dunce cap.

PRAISE IS A TRICKY BUSINESS IN LEARNING

In the beginning of this in-school period, praise is a very important part of the handling. Do not use food to show a dog what he is to do. Praise by voice and touch are fine during school. We have already talked about mealtime as an incentive or reinforcement of training, and a check on whether the dog understands the command. You will be able to tell if he is understanding you or is confused. If he's confused, let him eat; then go back to that lesson later. If he really knows the lesson, he should do it right . . . then be fed. We play this game even when dogs are adults.

The subject of praise with food is a very interesting one. In the show ring it is used to keep the dogs alert, and when the dog does well he gets a tidbit. Circus dogs are trained with food and when finished with their act receive a morsel from the trainer's pocket. A retriever should not work for food, and it will surprise you when I say that a working retriever should not work for praise once he has learned his job.

Jet, Tar's big brother, would sit and stay for a week if told to do so. But if I said, while he was sitting and staying, "That's a good boy!" and made a little fuss, he'd break and jump up and want to kiss. The praise seemed to take him off the hook—he couldn't handle it . . . praise "ends" the command.

THE STEPS IN LEARNING

Here are the steps in teaching a dog by the natural method:

1. Show the dog what the command means. This applies to both simple commands and advanced commands like directional handling by hand signals. Praise should be used when the dog shows he is trying to figure out what you want. Most people don't do a thorough job of showing a dog what is expected of him.

2. By repetition you embed the command into the dog. If he balks, start over and show him again what you want. Possibly try to make it easier. You are going to know when he understands what he is expected to do. When he does, add praise, then get the dog back to the "classroom" by commanding without praise. You will alternate this until you are sure he knows what you want. Once you are sure he knows what you want and he balks, then you can add discipline to the act, thus showing the dog that that is not what we want. Praise and reprimand will be important training tools.

3. Once the command is learned, stop giving him the praise. *The dog must learn to do the command for the sake of the work.* Watch a good worker bring in the duck; you will see that the doing is the reward. Save the praise for in front of the fireplace, when the work is over. Keep the work as commands.

We all know how to give praise, but sometimes a reprimand gets out of hand. We don't have to lose our tempers. Many times we lose them when it is not the dog's error. Save the big guns for a major problem later. Standing tall is itself a threat to a dog. They do not like to be towered over—add a disapproving voice and he'll put his tail between his legs. Most dogs need only one good whipping in their lives.

LIKE BUILDING BLOCKS . . . WE'LL BUILD

According to the animal behaviorists we are now in the final, the fifth, critical period of the pup's mental development. It will last for four weeks. Actually you will see, as we get into the next chapter, that this period runs to the twentieth week. The dog seems to come together mentally and physically at this point. At this time the pup is a gangly bundle of fur and seems puppyish in every way, but even now a lot can be accomplished by building on what we have started.

Let's extend him on command STAY. Sit the pup down in the middle of the yard. Command him to STAY. Then you walk backward toward the corner of the house. Give him one last STAY command and then duck around the corner . . . out of sight. Count to about five. Reappear. If he stayed for the five seconds, command STAY again and move out of sight and count ten. If he can't stand it another second and comes to find you, go back and start him all over again. A few days of this, building up the time, and he'll stay the rest of the week.

The fun about training a dog is that you do not have to tell him why he has to do this or that, as you do with a child. All the dog has to do is do it and "ask no questions." The next step in the building will come when we think the dog is ready.

Let's extend him, now, on COME, the command that will be used by the upland hunter and later in handling a blind. Your dog already knows the command in the controlled situation of the "class," be it in the house or yard. Now you will extend this to walks off the leash in a park or a field. He'll romp around, getting the good smells and having fun. That's when you start to train him to come back when you want. Start if you want by using the dog's name for attention, then immediately blow the come-in trill command. Make it fun and make a fuss over him when he does come. If he does not come, go to him and try it when you are close. If the pup gives you a problem and still won't obey, get to him and take him by the collar, walk him back to the place where he was when you first called, and start over. Don't let him get the idea that he can do this when he wants. He has to do it on command. But don't hack at him on your walks . . . let them be fun.

You are going to be way ahead of the game if you can control his range (his distance out in front of you) and not wait until these walks turn into the serious business of hunting later on. If he learns this range before he is actually hunting, your job will be made easier because in the field, with all the smells of game, a young dog will just go wild. But all those wonderful aromas will not give him the right to dash around the countryside like a madman busting the birds. If he does . . . he will know that he has done wrong, and why discipline is ahead in his near future.

CONSCIOUS AND UNCONSCIOUS LEARNING

Dogs can learn on two levels. When the dog is in class and is being taught the basic command SIT on whistle, that is a good example of conscious learning. He knows darn right well that school is in session. Learning distance limits on these early walks is a good example of unconscious learning. The dog is put into a situation repeatedly, in this case a specific distance from you, and he only gets the experience of being in that place or situation, it becomes natural for him. That is unconscious learning. There will be many things that you will not need to teach the dog if you handle him consistently. For example, I never have to teach a dog what side he is supposed to heel on. From the day he comes to me, he will walk only on the side I choose. He would feel uncomfortable any other place . . . now he just comes to that side.

As a dog gets bolder and bolder on these walks and wanders farther and farther, the come-in whistle will teach him shotgun range on this unconscious level. Never let him out of what you consider your gun range. For me, with the way I shoot, that's practically keeping the dog at heel!

MORE EXTENSION OF THE COMMANDS

During this period the command SIT or STOP (if the dog is in water) automatically turns into STAY. This was taught at heel, but now we extend it to any time or any place. This command separates the retrievers from the knotheads. On your walks off leash start him sitting on the one blast of the whistle when he is at heel. That's no problem—he learned that in the yard. The important building block is to have him obeying the command even when he is gadding about. You are asking him to do this while he has other interests on his mind.

Don't nag the pup, but spring the commands when he leasts expects it. If he fails to comply, gently make sure he understands he has to do what you want, not what *he* wants. Make him do it. This will save a lot of headaches later.

What you will be practicing will be for the handling to a blind retrieve later. The stopping is the first step. There is no real firmness in this at this time. It is all done as fun, while he is chasing the birds and bees . . . blast the SIT command. If he ignores you, get out there and make him do it. It won't take long for a pup to know what you want. Gradually increase the distance. A dog seems to learn that if he has put distance between the two of you, it is easier for him to thumb his nose at you. A dog senses this at a very tender age, so start close and build the distance gradually. That way you should be able to beat his act.

That reminds me of another dog named Tar that I was training when writing the book *Water Dog*. He was an exceptional fellow and took to his early training very well. He believed in me. But we got at odds one day while training with some friends. The test was one of his first blind retrieves and it was across a small river. I sent him on the blind from the bank and about half the way across he just took off in a new direction to do things his way (possibly he caught the sight or scent of something). I blasted for him to stop, to turn, paddle in "neutral," and then take my next directional signal to get him back on course. He stopped but refused to go the way I directed—off he went his way. I stopped him again . . . no way. He thought he knew better. Another stop . . . another refusal. Well, that is not the way things are supposed to work. I was convinced his big black head was thinking that there was not much I could do about it, since I was on land and he was in the water. I wondered if he knew that there was only one person who could walk on water, and although he liked me I was not that good.

I knew that if by some chance there was another bird out there and he got it on his own, not following my directions, a bad pattern would be set. I shed my shoes and wallet and dove in. Not hearing me come, when I got within arm's reach of him I blasted on the whistle. Tar spun around . . . eyes the size of saucers. "Holy cow! How did you get here?" was what his look said. I took him by the ears and dunked him . . . brought him up, blew one blast in his face . . . dunked him again. After about three dunkings and blasts we swam back to shore. Sopping wet, we started all over. That dog was great—he never again gave me the thumb or a refusal on land or water.

Of course this kind of a problem will come only later. At this time the STOP command will be taught only on land, so you can get to the pup if a correction is needed—short distances at first, because puppies do not have a long attention span. You do not want the dog to make an error, and then, by the time you get to him, be unable to remember what he was doing wrong.

The COME command will be important for the duck hunter also. It will be an important part of the handling later. When whistled to come back toward you he must comply. Later he will learn to follow the command and his reward will be a duck.

SWIMMING IS FOR RETRIEVERS AND DUCKS

How do you teach a dog to swim? How do you teach a duck to fly? They both come with the built-in instinct, if you don't mess it up. Some pups start right off at seven weeks if all situations are go; others don't start until they are five months old. Don't force the issue. Don't throw a pup in to swim or sink . . . why scare him?

Tar's response to water was typical. When he was just a little fellow of nine weeks, he'd play in the shallow water. He'd break thin ice and run the bank, but would not go in deeper than his chest. As the water got warmer and warmer he got bolder and bolder. He'd put his head under the water to retrieve a dummy and splash around having a good time. He already had a keen interest in dummies, so he'd stand barking at it if it was in water deeper than his belly. Oh, how he wanted it, but he just didn't have the nerve or know-how. (A good trick is to tie a string to the dummy so when you throw it in the water you can get it back if the pup isn't ready to do it for you.)

At twenty weeks all seemed to be right for Tar. The water was warm, he loved to retrieve on land, so I got out the fishing waders and decided to go in with him. The idea was to make a big fuss with a dummy, splash it around, and call the pup in with me. All the preparations were not needed. Dressed, ready to go, I made one last attempt. I threw a dummy into a stream that had a gradually sloping bed. Tar rushed in and before he even knew it he had taken three swimming strokes . . . and that was it. The next retrieve was 20 yards and the learning session was over . . . he became a fish.

Oh, how he wanted the dummy. He tried everything but swimming, . . . he just didn't have the nerve. He would break the ice, but when the water touched his belly he stepped back. No need to force this. It'll come.

I got Jet excited, then Tar. It was an easy walk-in beach. The dummy was thrown and that did it . . .

. . . pup Tar plowed in. Although I was ready to wade in and coax him, it was not necessary.

A pup will start to swim earlier if the body of water is not too wide. A small inlet is good, where the land is only a short distance in front of him. Entering a lake where the whole water expanse is ahead seems to be a problem. A pup will swim a 10-foot stream and refuse a lake until he learns that there is no real difference . . . you get wet in both.

He'll use a gentle mouth retrieving a firm brush. I've never known a dog to have hardmouth when started young. It seems that when they are started later, and can kill a bird, they do so after they have had a problem. Crunching the bird solves it and makes the job easier.

DUMMIES . . . DUMMIES . . . DUMMIES . . . AND MORE!

From day go, dummies are the name of the game. All through this in-school period the dog must get little retrieves as often as you have the time to play. If you can't spend more than two minutes before you are off to work . . . give him the two minutes. Make him love this and be just as crazy about it as food . . . like the drug-sniffing dogs.

Often when a very young pup is given his first bird to smell he'll stick his

Teaching a pup to use his nose after he's got the desire to fetch is easy. Throw the dummy into heavy cover. Let him mark the fall. Send him in; his nose will do the rest of the act.

neck out as far as possible to reach the smell, but the front legs stiffly hold him back and the back legs push him in. The whole body is ambivalent—the pup doesn't know which way to go. Not pup Tar; he had no fear . . . he figured that this was just one more of my environmental enrichment gimmicks. He charged the dead bird, figuring that I was giving him dinner. I stopped him immediately and decided that with his boldness I would teach him a thing or two. The next pheasant shot was still much alive when older Jet brought it in. It was flopping and flailing all over the ground. Before I could stop him, Tar was on the bird and finished him off . . . another dinner, he thought. I was concerned at his boldness, and he did not get another dead bird before he was bigger and had proved that he was a good retriever of dummies, and knew what I wanted him to do with them: deliver them to hand! In the meantime, I kept a dead pigeon in the freezer and we played with that quite often. If I did have a little fear of hardmouth at first, the frozen pigeon seemed to be the answer—he could not get his teeth into it. No one can be sure if that was the answer, but Tar had a fine mouth the first time he was sent for his own retrieve with a shot bird.

This is the period when the retrieve should be extended. At first it is very short and you play a teasing game around your feet; then it is made longer. First use a lawn so the pup can see everything. Then start throwing the dummy into the edge of the weeds and let him hunt a little. He will learn to use his nose. There is no use putting scent on the dummies—your own scent will be all he will need. Get the dog crazy to go.

HOLD . . . HOLD . . . HOLD! DROP YOUR TEETH BUT NOT THE BIRD!

If the pup has not learned earlier to bring the dummy to hand, and wants to play instead of deliver, as we discussed in the last chapter, you should do something about it now. Add this to it: run away from the pup as he comes toward you with the dummy . . . clap your hands . . . get excited, call him and add the command HOLD. Call excitedly, as you run away from him, "Come on, boy! Come on, Tar! HOLD! HOLD! Come on, boy!" When he gets behind you, and rather close, reverse your field. Turn and take the dummy out of his mouth and immediately throw it a short distance. When he picks it up, do your calling like a quarterback and your running like a halfback, reversing your field. The key to success in all this is your generating the excitement for the pup.

Many a bird that seemed stunned has flown off when a dog dropped it to shake off the water as he stepped onto land, or from between the hunter's legs as the dog dropped the bird at his master's feet. The command HOLD, for hand delivery, is something that does not come built into the dog as the retrieving instinct does. It has to be learned.

Tar never had the dropping problem because he was encouraged to hold things in his mouth at such an early age. Once I was sure he really wanted that dummy and was eager to retrieve. I started to have him pick the dummy up if he dropped it at my feet. This was easy to do while he was young. As he brought the dummy to me, I would encourage him by voice: "That's a good boy . . . good fellow!" If he dropped the dummy, I'd change my tone of voice and in a scolding way say, "Pick it up! Fetch it up!" I'd kick the dummy with my foot, so he was sure to know what I wanted, and repeat the command FETCH. When he picked up the dummy, I quickly took it out of his mouth and praised him. He soon got the idea of delivering to hand for the praise he wanted. Remember, do not start teaching HOLD until the desire to retrieve

Young dogs often develop the habit of dropping the bird before delivering, or after they come from the water and shake. Command HOLD while touching the jaw gets the point across. Slapping the jaw (right picture) will stop him from rolling the bird in his mouth. It may be necessary to put the dummy in the dog's mouth, then put both hands around his muzzle, and squeeze while commanding HOLD. This will be a struggle but you want him to learn that the word HOLD is associated with his mouth and the dummy. In water retrieves, get to the bank and command HOLD before he starts up on land.

has been highly developed—once this has been done, then HOLD can be built in.

The impulse to drop is strongest in most dogs when they come out of water. Even Tar did it, in spite of his early lessons. But it was easy to teach him to hand deliver from water, because he knew what pleased me. The way he was taught the command HOLD was to have him hold the dummy a few seconds, while retrieving on land, before I took it from him. I'd put my hand down as if to take the dummy but repeat the command several times before I actually took it from his mouth. Gradually the time of holding was increased. Then when it came to water it was simple. He knew the commands HOLD and PICK IT UP! FETCH IT UP!, so when he was returning by water, I got down to the water's edge and encouraged him for the retrieve he was making. When he got to within 6 feet of shore I'd command HOLD! At first he dropped it anyway to shake, but I scolded with, "FETCH IT UP! PICK IT UP!" When he did, the command HOLD was given. By repeating this, I got the idea across to him right away. But let's look ahead.

Sometimes the command HOLD does not go that smoothly. But this is not something to get upset about in a young dog, they outgrow the dropping habit if you do some teaching. If your pup is not doing it right at the age of about five months, open his mouth, put the dummy in and close it by using both hands around his muzzle. Hold the dummy there and keep repeating the HOLD command. That way he is surely going to learn what the word means. For practice, throw the dummy on the ground and command PICK

IT UP. If he won't, after a few commands are given, pick up the dummy and with a little force stick it in his mouth, commanding PICK IT UP! FETCH!, and hold it there with your hands and command HOLD! Actually you are teaching a simple version of force retrieve. Some dogs will fight this—fight back and show him who is boss.

Once the pup has learned this lesson, walk him at heel with the dummy in his mouth, commanding HOLD as you go. He will learn to like it. As we have said, young pups outgrow dropping, but hand delivery is a good thing to insist on, since it shows the pup that you really want "that thing" in his mouth, no matter what . . . and that is what a retrieve is all about. Once he learns that this is what you really want and that it pleases you, he won't balk at going back for a second retrieve just because the water is cold.

The command HOLD is much more than merely keeping slightly wounded game from flying off. It is as close as we shall get to force training, but it is important to teach the pup that you insist on his using his mouth . . . to fetch the game to you.

We have said that SIT, STAY, and COME are all-important, the name of the game in training a retriever. But the desire to retrieve goes hand in glove with the commands. The commands are taught as lessons; the other is developed as fun. What you are after, before the first twenty weeks are up, is to have the pup retrieving in water or on land as far as you can heave the dummy . . . and loving it.

THAT AWKWARD AGE

Starting at about the sixteenth week all retriever pups enter that gangly stage. Their legs are too long, their feet too big, their hindquarters taller than their shoulders, and they are bundles of energy. They are not cuddly things anymore and will go through that stubborn phase we parents know so much about. It too will pass. Then, this pup, if he has been handled properly, should have no fears . . . he'll be able to handle all kinds of new situations.

During the next four weeks or so the pup will be taught nothing new, but we shall firm up all we have shown him. He will do more of the same and will be expected to be rather sure of the basic commands by the time he is twenty weeks old. This is the time when pups are expected to become little ladies or gentlemen: housebreaking and chewing on furniture are things of the past . . . we hope. Jumping on people is a no-no. I do not mind too much if a pup jumps up on me; I'll bet it does not cost me ten dollars a year for dry cleaning, but it is not fair to have him jump on others. I usually have my wife or others train a dog not to jump up. The easiest way, when they are small, is to catch their legs and throw them over backward. When a dog is bigger, a knee in the chest to throw him off balance when he jumps up will do the trick. A few NO commands and he'll get the idea.

You are going to play all the fetch you can, but no sticks, balls, stones, or other stupid objects—use a dummy. Remember, no one should play tug-of-war unless you enjoy Chinese shredded duck Mow Pan Foo. About parlor games, leave them for the poodles. A retriever will have as much as he can handle learning his own game. Don't fill his head with nonsense.

HEEL IS FOR DOING . . . NOT CHEWING

The HEEL command should be started during this growing-up period. Your dog knows what the leash is all about. As he gets older and bolder he'll want to become the drum major, the leader of the band. He has to learn to stay back with the band and not be a wild Indian. He learns the command on leash . . . off later. Now is the time Tar had to learn to be a gentleman because he was starting to pull my arm out of its socket. It was easy, and it took only a one-mile walk.

I never use a metal choke collar—I like the nylon slip or choke collars better. I once had a dog's throat damaged using the metal one. The dog has always been on the side you chose when he first came with you. Often gunners like the dog on the side opposite which they carry their gun. Now you are ready to start your walk.

Tar started to pull immediately. He loved being the leader. I yanked

him and commanded HEEL. He more or less did it because I yanked him back to his position. Each time I yanked him I gave a firm HEEL. He got it when he moved in front of me, or to the side, sniffed, yanked, lagged, or stopped. But it was especially when he put pressure on my end of the leash that I put big pressure on his end. It must have taken three hundred or eight hundred yanks, or some such, in the mile walk . . . and I had a sore hand. But at the end of the walk he was walking like a gentleman . . . at my side and no pulling. The next time out he only had to be reminded, and then he settled into his place.

WORKING TWO DOGS TOGETHER

If you are planning to work your pup with another dog, as I did with the pup, Tar, and five-year-old Jet, they have to learn to work together. The best way to get across the idea that one stays at heel while the other one is to work is to start at this age feeding them together and doing it by name. Now that you have the pup to a point where he will sit and stay on command, you are ready to start this training. I got the two pans of food prepared and then called them to heel. Jet heeled on my left, pup Tar on the right. While they sat and stayed, I walked forward and put the two pans down. Then I called them one at a time. One came to eat and the other one waited a few seconds before he was called. One night Jet got it first; Tar got it first the next night. When Tar was ten months old, I took them both to a tower shoot, and the pup did what I expected him to do . . . he didn't break. He could hardly contain himself—but he waited his turn!

I never seriously train for the command HEEL until the pup gets to size. Before that I make sure that when he is on leash, he is always on the side he will be trained to. He'll learn his place because he is never in any other position. Teaching HEEL depends on the dog. The knothead who wants to be the leader of the band has to be yanked under control. Many dogs do better off leash. I hold the training strap so he can see it and just touch him with it when he forgets his place. I do not subscribe to the formal obedience method. It is too exacting. I guess it is because I have never seen a good working retriever come out of obedience schooling.

Although I believe it is simpler for the hunter to train one dog at a time, working a pair of retrievers is a pleasure. Ideally, I like one dog to be five years old when I start a pup. That way, if something happens to the older dog, there is a young dog right behind him. Losing a well-trained, only dog is a tragedy. Having two dogs gives a sort of protection.

FEEDING TIME IS MORE THAN FOOD

What you feed your dog is between you and your vet, but I'd like to get in the act on *how* you feed him. Some dog people object to using mealtime as I do, but I think they mix up what food is to us humans and what it is to the dog. We people like to sit over a meal and have good conversation and a fine wine. My dogs eat like vacuum cleaners.

We all work for our bread, and I see no reason for a dog to be any different. We have just talked about using the food to learn to wait while another dog does his work. We do something every evening . . . and they expect it. If I'm teaching the pup to bring the dummy to hand during the day, I'll try him on it at mealtime to see whether, through all the excitement of the best part of the day, he understands and remembers the work. I feel the dog has to be kept on his toes, and it is important to keep building the rapport between you. The dog sure gets to know that you are the one who feeds him, and food is a good way to keep that bond going.

When I hunt the dogs or have a good training session I do not do the "game-playing" at supper time . . . they have done their work for the day. Otherwise, just as blessing the food is a ritual at mealtime, response to your command is the dog's food ritual, for the rest of his life.

Tar is only twenty weeks old—that's only 140 or so days old. That is very young, but with the care and direction we have given him he has surely become a responsible little fellow. I'm not sure any pup I've worked with has been more responsive. He has been a keen and fast learner, with enthusiasm and a desire to work. He has even taken his scoldings like a little man. One reaction he has is to sit at heel when I scold him, and his lower jaw seems to quiver . . . and I know it's not with fear. What he wants to do is go again. He never wants to quit.

How far do you take the pup during this period? A smart trainer lets the dog set the pace. With Tar, I was so sure that he would not break the SIT command when he was at heel that I started to have him wait for me to release him when I threw the dummy. Right from this early age, he learned not to break. That's something the field trialers would throw up their hands at . . . "That would ruin a dog at that age!" . . . Didn't ruin Tar!

Chapter 6

Vocational School Begins

TWENTY WEEKS . . . THE DIVIDING POINT

Our grandfathers and great-grandfathers were apprenticed out at a very early age to learn a trade. That is not socially accepted today, but what evolved back then was a skilled work force of craftsmen and artisans. That society carved things by hand; today we stamp them out. They knew back then that to achieve the needed skills, early training was necessary.

In observing the mental and physical development of young retrievers, it has been my experience that twenty weeks is the dividing point in the hunting retriever's education. At that age, about five months, the pup is ready and eager to embark upon the advanced stages of his training as a hunting dog. If he has been brought along this far step by step, he will make a fine hunter at about one year of age.

Of course, we are going to proceed slowly; your dog is not going to be ruined, as we have been told for decades. The old writers who held to that axiom would be hard pressed to explain what Tar has already accomplished by this time. They didn't know because they didn't try. The "ruination" test is simple and you can run it yourself . . . and you should be doing this all the way through the training. A dog cannot hide its "feelings," and you can tell the minute things are going wrong or he's confused. His tail will show all. If it's up and the dog is perky, do you believe the dog is being ruined?

Let's put down another age-old excuse the hunter has been using; "I do not have the time to do all this." That is just a cop-out for not knowing how to proceed or what to do step by step. Like many of you, I go to an office every day and business often takes me away from home. It is a logical progression from here on out that makes for success, and a few days skipped one way or the other are not going to be that important. With that understood, let's tick off what we have accomplished at this point: Tar is a happy pup . . . he knows SIT, STAY, COME by voice and whistle and does them rather consistently off leash. He loves to play fetch. The dummy is a big part of his life and scores second only to eating. He has had all kinds of experiences and has no fears of the big world around him. He is bold and loves to travel. He knows his place around the house . . . understands and respects the command NO. The noise of a gun is music to his ears. He walks like a gentleman on leash and knows the command HEEL even though he does not do it too well off lead. Because we played fetch so early, he will deliver a dummy to hand and, surprisingly, he did not have to be taught as such—he just learned it. He swims like an otter and will keep going back to retrieve until my arm is tired. (Most pups start swimming by arching their backs to keep their heads up; in that position their paws beat the water, splash, and they get nowhere.) Tar started right off like an adult dog. On land, Tar is smelling all sorts of good things and chasing the butterflies . . . he picks up downed game and likes that. The most important thing, however, is that he has learned to learn and has mastered the important lessons at this age, SIT, STAY, COME, and playing fetch. If he hadn't learned these lessons well, I would not have taken him further until he had.

LET'S BE HONEST . . . WHAT IF YOU START LATE?

We have not said too much up to this point about the fellow who gets the dog late and then gets ahold of this book. What does the guy do who had always heard that you do not start the training until the dog is six months old or older? About that time he decides to buy a book and it tells him he has wasted the valuable time. He has three choices: First, he can say he does not believe all this early stuff I've been writing and throw the book away. Second, he can give the dog away and start over . . . and at the same time look for a new wife and kids who won't hate him. Third, he can follow the procedure outlined for the pup and apply it to the older dog. He is going to have to get to the point we have Tar at (the twenty-week point) before he can proceed. It might take a baseball bat to get the dog's attention, and miles of patience. He'll have to be a psychologist and a bit of a magician, but with kindness and a firm hand the job can be accomplished—it is just the hard way. So many hunters say that they do not have the patience to train. Actually what they are saying is that they have run into a problem and do not know how to get out of it—the dog won't heed commands unless he wants to, or won't retrieve, or doesn't like birds, or thumbs his nose at you when he is off having a good time doing things his way. These problems are aggravating for the amateur, and patience testers. Little patience is needed when you build early, from scratch—mistakes are easy to correct, attitudes easy to develop—but all this *can* be done with an older dog; many hunters have done it. You are not the first by any means to start with an older dog . . . so stick at it and try.

A NEW APPROACH TO THE HUNTER'S NEEDS

As we have seen, most of what you have read on training a retriever has been written with the field-trial game in mind, and traditional training is based on that game. It is just not the hunter's game. It is true that a good field-trial dog will make an excellent hunting dog. The dog will quickly learn our game. But the traditional way of training, with its very slow time schedule, will waste a lot of time for the hunter. We shall not assume that you know field trials and shall explain that difference, as we go along, to help you understand your job. For starters, you should know that the field-trial work does not include any upland hunting. The dog is given no opportunity to track a bird, and in some ways is discouraged from using his nose.

Next, as you proceed you should keep your particular job in mind —whether you are going to be basically a waterfowl or an upland hunter, or both. The reason for having to know this is a very simple one. We play two different hunting games with our retrievers for the different species of birds . . . and we do not want to cause any confusion. Here is an example of what that means. In a waterfowl situation the dogs learns never to come back without a bird—that is a no-no. Even if the dog did not see the bird downed, he is not to come back until he has worked out the problem and tracked the bird. *In that situation we know darn right well the bird is there.* In upland work, if we send a dog into a piece of cover, *we both can only hope that a bird is there.* If no bird is there, we want the dog, after he has made a search, to come back to the handler or go on hunting in a new direction. The dog has to learn when you want him to hunt out a dead bird or when you want him to see if a live one is there. I've seen well-trained duck dogs return to their handlers on whistle, from a piece of upland cover, with their tails between their legs. Dogs must learn that they are playing two different games. The upland dog hunts on his own, under certain controls . . . the waterfowl dog hunts strictly under the guidance of the hunter. In one case he is expected to leave the cover if he does not find the bird, and in the other he can't leave the cover until he does find it. This can be confusing to a young dog. So, to get around the confusion, we shall use different commands for the two types of hunting jobs. Then you can use the dog for both kinds of work. I like to get a young dog trained to his duck work first, before I put him on the upland birds. As you will see, the duck work is much more exacting. A lot of the upland work is instinct . . . waterfowling is instinct plus control.

THE MARKED FALL

The field-trial dog, to be worth his weight in dog food, has to be an excellent marker with a memory as good as his handler's is. That means that the dog will see the fall of game and pinpoint the mark, remember as many as three marks, and sometimes be required to work as many as five. It is uncanny to see him do this. It takes a lot of work, day after day, and lots of assistance. To get this kind of precision means endless hours and great expense—understandably this turns off the hunter. There is no question that this kind of accuracy is required to win a field trial, but how often does this situation occur for the hunter? When was the last time you had a double . . . or when was the last time three, four, or five birds were dropped from a blind you were in? But more important, if that many birds were down, is it the responsibility of the dog alone to remember the falls? No matter how good the dog is, the man is better. But, and this is an important *but*, in so many of the real hunting situations the dog never sees the birds go down. How can he see them when he is sitting in a blind?

The field-trial method of taking the dog to the *line* (starting place), where the handler and the dog can see every fall, is artificial. Standing out on a mound, in the open for God and all the ducks to see, isn't conducive to bringing in the birds. We just do not hunt that way.

When we consider the hunting situation, it does not seem logical for the hunter to go through this precise memory-training procedure. It is not needed. What we want is to have the dog be able to do long, difficult singles. Eventually a dog will work up to about 200 yards over difficult terrain. Then, when that dog is put on live game in real situations and becomes "birdy," he will teach himself doubles or triples. He'll learn to watch the birds and will soon know which are hit and which aren't. He learns to play the game and will watch the falls. If he is birdy and loves to retrieve, it will come with experience. The thing that is vital is that if the dog is outside the blind and in a position to see all the falls, he should not move until the action is over so he can see it all.

There is another part of trials that is unnatural for the hunter. For birds to be shot by guns 150 yards and farther away for a dog to mark them down is not the way it happens in most hunting situations. It might occur on that rare occasion when your dog is covering for two blinds. What the trial setup is supposed to simulate is the bird that is winged and glides down and then

Jet knew the first time he hunted from a box outside the blind what the game we were playing was. He observed everything that was happening in the sky. Doubles? No one had to teach him!

dumps in. Actually the hunter's dog has to learn to follow the bird that is wounded, track that long flight, and mark where the bird tumbles out of the sky.

If a bird is shot in a trial, is not hit clean, and sails off, the situation is called *no bird*. The dog is taken off line and rerun later. All dogs must have the exact same test, and a winged bird is considered a disadvantage. (That is understandable because the dog may take half an hour to make such a retrieve and to run a hundred dogs in a day would be impossible. No way could that shot be duplicated for all the other dogs, even if time were not a factor.) This means that a field-trial dog in the United States (they do track in England) could become a field-trial champion and never have to learn or demonstrate that he can track a cripple.

So, in our training, we shall eliminate the time-consuming memory development, train for single retrieves, have the dog learn doubles, triples, or more by experience, and teach the dog to track crippled game.

THE SINGLE RETRIEVE . . . ITS ELEMENTS

At twenty weeks Tar was ready to get serious about this business. By the time he was six months old he was rather accurate. He had to SIT at heel on the one blast of the whistle. He had to STAY until the dummy was thrown. He waited until a hand signal showed him the direction to go, the two blasts were given, and then he went a-flying. Gradually the distances were increased. The task was made harder. Those early retrieves were all "sight" retrieves. When he would go as far as I could send him on a grassy field, it was made more difficult by using weedy cover where he would have to use his nose. In this more difficult cover the retrieves were shortened to get all the odds working on his side. This meant he was starting to use his nose to find the dummy, and not his eyes, and was obliged to hunt out the dummy. Gradually the distances were increased once again, and his marking ability improved, and so did his nose.

One thing we never allowed to happen was for him to give up. I felt lucky with Tar because he never seemed to want to quit. I believe that came from two factors: one, he did have good working stock in his bloodlines, and second, making him crazy to play fetch early paid off . . . it kept him going, kept him hunting. Whenever he hunted too long and worked himself out of the area, I'd run out and give him a hand. I'd call him back to the area and we would both hunt up the dummy until he found it. But he did not come to depend on me for this help. On introducing the weedy cover, first only its edge was used. When he became successful in finding the dummy, the throws were made deeper and deeper into the heavy stuff.

One thing you must be ready for and that is the first sign of the pup's not finding the bird and giving up. Don't let him come back to you without it. If you were not smart enough to help him when he got into trouble, then you have put yourself into a box. If he comes back without it, you have to scold him. Run at him as he comes back without it. Make a lot of noise . . . flail your arms . . . holler "NO! NO!" Make sure he knows that that is not what you want. Run out and help him. Don't be too friendly with him until you are both coming back with the dummy in his mouth. Get friendly with him and do it again. If this happens again . . . shake him up! Let him know we can't have that sort of thing. Again, like the command HOLD, this is a simple version of force training.

Long retrieves were accomplished in two ways. On occasions when I had a helper, I'd have him stand out on the edge of a field, and after the helper got the pup's attention by calling, he'd throw the dummy for him to retrieve. I'd send the dog by two blasts of the whistle. Gradually the helper would be sent out farther and farther, making the retrieves longer and longer, and at the same time taking advantage of all sorts of terrain. This would simulate the later conditions when Tar would be working for hunters in two separate blinds (tracking birds shot at a distance). The problems with that are twofold. Having a guy stand out in a field has nothing to do with duck hunting. The dog will learn to mark the area within the throwing distance of the helper. There will be no helper during hunting season. The other problem is that getting helpers is not that easy. With these two facts in mind, I came on the idea and then codesigned the first dummy launcher some twenty years ago. Either I would use the launcher with the dog at heel or have the dog SIT, STAY, walk away a few yards or more, and then fire it. The dog has to learn that you are not always standing right at his side, field-trial style. In hunting situations the dog often has to sit outside as the guns take cover. The dummy launcher gives the dog real training in eye tracking.

The same gradual procedure was used with water retrieves. They were made longer and longer and then on water and land combined. The idea is to get the dog used to going into the water, then up on land to hunt. Again, this was first done by sight. By first throwing the dummy on the edge of the opposite bank where he could see it the whole time he was swimming, we made it very simple for the pup. Then the dog was required to go farther and farther up on the bank until finally the heavier cover was introduced on the opposite shore—he'd have to hunt once he had swum to the opposite bank.

Teaching long single retrieves is straightforward. As Tar would learn one thing, it was extended to the next step. There are only two no-nos in this work. One is the pup's giving up, and the other is the pup's getting out of the hunting area, the area of the fall. On the first the dog is scolded, as we have just discussed, and made to go back again to keep on hunting. I believe I had to run out with Tar only once because he quit, and I wasn't very friendly about it until he "discovered" the dummy. Then I gave him praise to show that that was what I wanted. The other problem, getting out of the area of the fall, should not be treated as a wrong, but with a "Come on, you good fellow, don't be so stupid" attitude. Call him to you as you run out to the area of the fall. When you get there, stop and tell him to fetch it up. He'll search and find—then give him praise. In either case, start over with another retrieve from the beginning point and into the same area. Do it over until he gets the idea of what you want.

Dummy throwers are very useful gadgets for the trainer who does not have helpers. Singles, doubles, or triples can be put out as far as 100 yards. This teaches the dog to track a moving object and mark it down, and the sound of the gun comes built in. It makes placing blind retrieves a simple matter. It is also a fun way for the dog to get exercise and stay in condition.

THE DUMMY LAUNCHER . . . A TOOL TO HELP EXTEND THE DOG

The plastic-and-steel Dummy Launcher is the latest launching device for retriever dummies. It could be considered the third generation in the development of this tool. It is an excellent gadget for those who train without a helper. The gas from .22 blank ammunition powers the launch, and distances can be regulated with different power levels of ammo.

The unit teaches a young dog to track a moving object and has the sound of the gun. The retrieves can be made on water or land. The dummies float and they are not damaged if they hit a hard object. Multiple retrieves can be

The dummy launcher has an easy grip, space-age handle of polycarbonate with a soft foam rubber recoil pad. Its steel spud makes it look like a gun but it is not considered a firearm.

made by using two or three dummies. The launcher makes the setting out of blind retrieves a simple matter. With the dog out of sight, the launch can be made without the dog knowing where it falls. Then the dog can be brought to the launch area and sent with the controls of hand signals and whistle to retrieve the "blind." For the hunter this is the work that separates the men from the boys. A dog that can do a blind retrieve is a real conservationist.

A most important use of this tool is to extend a young dog. When thrown dummies are used, without an assistant, the dog learns to go the distance the trainer can throw the dummies. The launcher extends the dog and teaches him he has to go out seventy-five or more yards.

The idea for this device came to me while watching a woman run her dog in a club training session. She had a fine dog but he only ran out twenty or so yards and started to search for the dummy that had been thrown fifty yards out. Later she told me she had a twenty-yard dog because she trained alone and could only throw the dummy that short distance. That was thirty years ago and that's when the idea was born for the first launcher.

The first unit, called Retriev-R-Trainer, had one drawback: The handle had no protection for the hand. If not held very tightly, the hand could be shoved against the metal by the force of the shot. It could produce some

The variety of dummies are either heavy-duty canvas-covered nylon Cordura or oval-shaped PVC plastic. The center bottom dummy has a tail that is supposed to give it a birdlike flight.

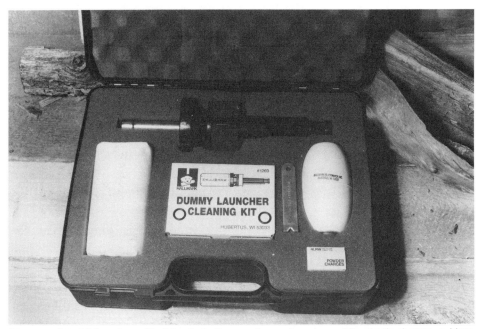

The complete kit in a foam-fitted hard plastic case has a launcher, white plastic dummy, a blaze orange nylon dummy, a box of ammo, cleaning kit, shell extractor, and replacement "O" rings.

The best throw dummies are 2" by 12" in a soft plastic that stays flexible in cold weather, are ideal for water retrieves, and are easy to keep clean. They come in 3½" but the 2" is easier to carry and store. They come in white, black, and fluorescent orange, which a dog sees as gray.

pretty good bruises, even cuts. This third-generation launcher has a strong plastic hand grip with a foam collar that protects the hand from the kick of the gun.

Dummies are available in many different shapes. Some are all plastic and some are foam plastic covered in canvas. I like the all-plastic dummies best. The canvas-covered ones can get grimy and can have an unpleasant odor after getting wet in a swamp. The all-plastic, oval-shaped ones do not put up as much resistance to the air and fly farther.

Color is important. White dummies are used because the dog can see them on the ground. It is good to use white ones with a young dog while you are extending his distance. White dummies help him. Because dogs are color-blind they cannot see the red or orange dummies as well; they see them as shades of gray. Many trainers like this because a dog can almost be on top of the dummy and not see it. This teaches the dog to use his nose.

It has been thought by some trainers that when the sky is very bright the dog does not see the white dummies against the sky. They have asked to have black dummies made, which they feel helps solve that problem.

You can use the launcher along with throw dummies. Shoot out a long one. Then throw one to the right and one to the left, long and short. By instinct a dog goes to the last dummy down. He will pick up the two short ones, the last two down . . . then see if he remembers where the long first one was shot. This is how you develop the dog's memory.

It is a good idea to use ear plugs while using a launcher. Do not start off with the dog at your side for the first few shots. The .22 blanks have a sharp crack that is unlike the boom of a shotgun. Let the dog get used to the sound by standing off a few yards in the beginning.

DUMMY LAUNCHER
The Dummy Launcher, the improved Retriev-R-Trainer, and accessories can be purchased from Hallmark Dog Training Supplies (3054 Beechwood Ind. Court, Hubertus, WI 53033; telephone 414-628-2500; fax 414-628-4434) or from your local Hallmark Dog Training Supplies dealer.

#1230 Launcher only (no dummy)

PVC plastic dummy, 5" long by 3" wide
#1251 White Plastic
#1252 Red Plastic

Nylon dummy, 6½" long by 3" wide
#1257 White Cordura Nylon with Streamer
#1260 White Cordura Nylon
#1261 Camouflage Cordura Nylon
#1262 Blaze Orange Cordura Nylon

Blank Ammunition . . . color coded, 100 per box
#1263 #3 Green light load, 150 feet
#1264 #4 Yellow medium load, 200 feet
#1265 #5 Red heavy load, 250 feet

#1275 Complete launcher kit with case

Write or call for a complete retriever training supply catalog and price list.

Note how the launcher is held. The holding hand crosses in front of the body. The recoil is taken up by the crossing arm, which acts like a shock absorber.

A dog has to be set up at heel with his eyes, head, and spine pointed in the right direction. The hand shows the way. Reheel him if he is not pointed correctly.

SET THE DOG UP STRAIGHT

When you are going to send the dog for a retrieve for waterfowl work he should be set up properly. The dog is at heel, on the same side he has always been on. Then he is commanded with the whistle to SIT. The line of his spine should point directly to the fall. The dog's head should be also in that straight line—he should be looking in the direction in which he is going to go. If you can't seem to get him to sit the way you want. start over . . . walk him around and then sit him again. Once he is lined up with the correct place, put your hand, thumb up, in front of his face to point the way. When all is set give the two whistle blasts to GO. As you do this move your hand forward as if guiding him in the right direction. That hand and arm movement is not a big motion. Many new handlers make this motion a "whoosh," pulling their hand behind the dog's head and then throwing it forward . . . as if they were pushing the dog. This is wrong, because the dog cannot see that arm coming from behind his head.

With a young pup just starting, the hand shows the way even if the dummy is in full view. That the hand shows the way will become most important later, so why not teach it from the start?

This setting up and hand direction is all very important for later use. With a young pup, even if the dummy is only 20 feet away on a grassy lawn and can be seen with ease, the line-up and hand direction should be given to teach the dog, on something that is obvious, what the hand directional signal means. Later, when he can't see where the dummy is, that line-up and hand means to go straight out, and it will be there.

I'll even set the pup as if he were doing a retrieve when I feed him. The pan is down . . . he sees it . . . from heel he will be sent on command to his food with the hand showing the way. As if he needs that!

DECOYS ARE FOR THE DUCKS . . . NOT THE TABLE

When the pup is still young and the weather is right, why not introduce him to decoys? I've seen many a young fellow, during his first season, proudly try, for all he was worth, to bring in the blocks, anchor and all, back to the blind. Also, many a young dog has been spooked by the decoys. It is easy to get the dog to ignore the stool . . . unless he's a woodhead himself.

Lay half a dozen decoys on the lawn and walk the dog through them. Let him smell them. He won't have much to do with them. Then walk him away . . . throw a dummy into the center of the blocks. Let him retrieve. Throw the dummy past the decoys so he has to run through them. He'll do it without any problem. Then do this in water. Put the decoys in the water on individual strings and send the dog for some dummies in and around them. If the pup gets tangled, encourage him to keep going. Some dogs panic when they get tangled in the lines . . . that is why it is best to have them on separate anchors until they learn that they won't get hurt.

"What's that? . . . Looks good enough to eat."

Don't wait till opening day to teach your retriever the difference between decoys and ducks, unless you like eating painted wood.

He'll learn immediately to ignore the blocks on land and will do the same thing in water. The water rig should have each decoy attached to a single line and anchor. A young dog getting caught in and dragging a string of decoys can be frightened.

WALKING THE PLANK

While still at this early age the dog should be introduced to the boat—not only getting into one but also getting out. A boat on the beach or at a dockside is not a normal thing for a dog to deal with. A rocky boat and

Start 'em young around boats. The footing is different; the rocking motion will be new. Don't wait for opening day, with all the gear, to teach this. I have a duck-hunting friend who feels sick every time we go in a boat. I guess his mother started him too late.

strange underfooting can be frightening. It is best to do this before the season starts so that the introduction can take as long as the pup needs to be comfortable getting in and out. When everyone is in a hurry, opening morning is the wrong time to try to get this chore learned.

The easiest way, if the dog is reluctant, is to get into the boat yourself and call the dog to you. At first, try to hold the boat steady. Have him get in and out a number of times until he seems to have no problem. Hold onto the pup when you cast off and start the motor. We anchored and then threw a dummy overboard. On command, Tar went over the side and made the retrieve. At first he slithered over the gunwale and it hurt me more than

Throw the dummy. Splat! If the dog is crazy about retrieving, he'll figure he must walk the plank. Bottoms up, but be careful of the "hook"!

him—I thought he'd caught his "hook." He soon learned to dive over the side!

Getting him back in the boat is more of a chore. The first thing to do is to take the dummy or bird from the dog's mouth, or he'll crunch down on it when straining to get back in. Let the dog swim and call him to you. When he tries to climb up the side of the boat, put your hand behind his neck, and with that pressure he may be able to make it back in. If the gunwale is too high, place one hand on the back of his neck, grab the skin on his rump, and heave-ho.

It took Tar just a few retrieves to learn to go overboard with style.

Getting him back in can be a problem for both of you. The dog will swim back to the boat. While he is swimming, lean over and take the dummy or bird out of his mouth. It will be a strain getting back in the boat, and he'll chomp down and crush his bird. Coax him to you. Let him try to climb back in. In a low boat let him get his feet over the gunwale, put your hand behind his neck. With that pressure he can climb in. In a high boat, when he tries to climb in, grab his collar and heave-ho. Suggest he go below to shake!

This is the time in a pup's learning to make sure you get him accustomed to any special ways that you hunt, such as with the boat. Let me give you an example of how I goofed with Tar. When he became eleven months we were invited to go goose hunting. Before sunrise we were all out setting up the rig around the pit blind. Once we finished we went about getting guns, ammo, coffee, milkshakes, extra clothes, and all the rest of the junk into the pit. When we were all assembled, waiting for the clock to announce the time to begin, and of course the prayer for the geese, my host announced that he would feel better if the dog were in the pit. I'd never hunted that way and had never given Tar that experience. Although we had flashlights to show the dog what the pit was all about—no way he was going into that hole. He sat outside, next to the pit, and that was that.

If you hunt snow geese in an open field in Texas, and use white sheeting as decoys, don't wait until opening day to try to teach a pup to lie down with a white cloth over him—it won't work. Do it around the house. Make him learn to stay with the cloth on his back. I know one hunter who made a white cover for his dog that had light Velcro on it to keep it in place. A string was attached to the cover and tied to a bush . . . when the dog was sent, the cover stayed behind.

Whatever it might be . . . sitting on a stump . . . sitting quietly in a blind . . . sitting on a platform under a water blind . . . no matter what, off season and when he is young is the time to get the dog used to what is going to be expected of him. As Dr. Fox says . . . environmental enrichment!

BIRDS AND GUNS . . . THAT'S WHAT IT IS ALL ABOUT

The period in the training following the pup's first twenty weeks is the time when all sorts of goodies happen. This does not mean that they all come at the same time, but all these new experiences start to happen when the pup is five or six months old. Of course Tar had had birds before his twentieth week. He knew the smells and, as we have said, had no fears at all. At about five months he was given his first shot pigeons. A friend handled the gun and birds and I handled the pup. The birds were thrown, shot, and landed in heavy cover.

It was a most thrilling time for Tar. The pigeons added all sorts of excitement, and when the first one flew and the gun went off only 25 yards away . . . he flew too. All he had learned went on fleeting wings. But one blast of the whistle brought him back to earth and he jammed on the brakes and stopped. He remembered! He turned and sat, then came back to heel on the whistle. That controlled break wasn't bad for such a young fellow. Then in high gear he was off to make the retrieve when I sent him. He remembered his manners for the rest of the birds we shot for him.

It was just a matter of putting all the elements together for Tar. He had been introduced to the gun and game. He at first had the dead birds thrown for him so he knew how to handle them. The gun was no problem and the control commands were in his head. Pigeons shot over water were no different . . . he handled them too.

Live birds often trouble young dogs. If pups are not put on live ducks before they get into a field trial you often find that they will not handle a shackled duck. A pecking, quacking duck can be formidable. Most dogs get over this with experience. The sad thing is to see an older dog without experience run out and go to a bird but refuse to retrieve it. What do you do? Pray, then start over from the beginning and see what happens. It is not easy.

TRACKING . . . USING THE HERITAGE

For the upland hunter, tracking is a must. Retrievers have excellent noses, and this ability should come built in from mom and dad. A young dog that has been made birdy will have no trouble learning this one. The setting should be a big field with a road cut through it. You take a duck and shackle its wings so it cannot fly. Put your dog at heel and have an assistant show the bird to the dog. With the dog at your heel, the assistant starts to walk down the road carrying the duck so the dog can see it. At 50 to 75 yards the duck is set down on the road and the assistant moves out of the way quickly. The duck will waddle around and then walk into the cover. All this time the pup is beady-eyed watching that bird. Let the bird wander off into the cover. Make the dog wait. After five minutes release the dog. He'll run down the road and cut into the cover; he has to use his nose to track the bird.

Then the fun begins. Tar enjoyed this game. He was so good at it. He learned to circle and home in on the bird and you could tell by his movements when he had scent and when he lost it. This game is extended and the bird is given plenty of time to wander off. The dog will learn to work out the problem—tracking is as natural to retrievers as carrying. This is something that the field-trial dogs never get a chance to demonstrate . . . but they would be good at it.

Command SIT. Show him the bird . . .   . . . Walk away and plant the bird . . .

... Let the pheasant run off ...

... Go back and wait until the bird is gone ...

... The dog will be some excited. Send him ...

... He'll rush to the area. No bird! ... turn page!

... The hunt is on. He may start by sight ...

... then circle the area to pick up scent ...

... Tar tracks the bird down. As he gets better ...

... and better, extend the waiting time.

QUARTERING . . . THE UPLAND GAME

My own preference is not to start a young dog on upland work until he is firm on his duck-hunting commands. I do not like the idea of the possible confusion that might arise from hunting on his own in upland work as opposed to the control I want for the waterfowl hunting. I am sure I could be proved wrong on this . . . a smart young dog could handle both. I waited until Tar was eleven months old before he hunted upland in front of the guns. The results of his first hunt were no less than spectacular. By that time he was rather seasoned as a retriever, having brought in literally hundreds of training and game birds working from my side. The waterfowl hunter should make his own determination when to start the upland work.

For the upland hunter the trick, the name of the game, is to get started as soon as possible. All the training that led up to the twenty-week point would be the same for both kinds of work. After twenty weeks, no matter what the season, the dog should be in the fields and woods as much as possible.

When he was a wee pup we got Tar out in the fields and he walked in my tracks, practically on my heels. Remember we always turned to face the dog, no matter in which direction he walked and frolicked. That was to keep him out in front. This should continue, as he gets bolder and ranges out, until you get the idea that he has gotten the idea as to where he should be: *in front of you.* Now Tar is a bold fellow and is always out ahead.

THE UPLAND COMMANDS

As previously mentioned, we shall use a set of commands just for the upland work. The reason was explained earlier in this chapter—it is to avoid confusion with the waterfowl work. The upland commands we shall use are better suited for upland hunting anyway.

HUNT 'EM UP will be used to send the dog off to start his quartering. The hand signal that goes with this command is a general sweep of the arm that says this is the way to go.

COME AROUND will be used to turn the dog when he is on a cast to the side and bring him around to start his swing in front of you toward the other side. The arm signal will be a sweeping motion to the right or left. It's pointing in the new direction. Use the left arm to the left and the right to the right. Make a motion with your body and walk in that direction as you give the signal. That is to signal him that you are going in that direction and he should come along . . . or else. (More on this shortly.)

GET IN . . . GET IN will be the command to have the dog investigate a good, birdy piece of cover. You will point to the cover and direct him in. (More on this, too.)

WHISTLE TRILL, the COME command that he has learned, will be used to bring him back into gun range when he gets out too far. (This is a backup to the COME AROUND command.)

ONE BLAST will be the STOP command that he has learned. This will be used to stop the dog on the flush of the game.

A word about giving the commands: Some hunters do not like a lot of chatter when they hunt. I suggest that you have them hunt with someone else until your dog really learns his job. You will want to keep giving your young dog directions. His mommy may have given him the desire to hunt, but she forgot to include in her genes the "how." You will want the young dog always to know that you are there to oversee things. He has to do all this for you, not himself. How do we start?

STARTING UPLAND WORK

The early walks are doing more than giving the pup the new experience of woods and fields. At first he'll stay behind you. It is easier for him to walk in your tracks than to forge his own way in the stubble. As he stays on your heels, lift your shoe high and clobber him gently a few times on the jaw. He learns to stay his distance. He follows by dropping back a yard. That's the last time the dog will ever be behind you. Once he drops back, you turn and now he is in front of you. Wherever he goes, you now face him. He will learn that his place is in front of you. He will get bolder and go off on his own, but from now on it will be out in front. He learns his place . . . out front where a hunting dog should be.

THE ZIGZAG IS FOR DRUNKS AND YOUNG RETRIEVERS

You will want the dog to learn to quarter the whole field and cover as much of it as possible—from shotgun range on one side to gun range on the other. So you will start this in any field, be it a lawn or bird cover. You will walk the path you expect the dog to run by himself later. Cast the dog off with the HUNT 'EM UP command and walk off toward the right side of the field. With the dog in front, you will let him charge around having his fun. If he goes to get behind you, you will command COME AROUND and give the appropriate arm signal. When he gets to the edge of the field, give the COME AROUND command. You turn and walk in the new direction and with your arm point the way with the sweeping motion. Keep encouraging the young dog to go on. At the left border of the field turn him again, the same way you did it on the other side. You will be walking a zigzag and the dog will be running it.

Once you feel the dog is getting the drift you can start to cut down the length of your zig and zag. The end of the line is for you to be walking a straight line, while the dog will zigzag covering the whole course . . . after all he has four legs and you only two.

We shall use more voice commands here because the distances will not be that great. This does cut down on the noise, but more important, it gives you the whistle as the backup for the COME AROUND command. If he does not come around to the voice command, use the whistle to show him you mean business. As the dog progresses, and when you think he knows what the whole thing is about, you can shake him up if he gets too far out and is not paying attention to the whistle. This is the no-no in this game. He must stay within gun range. Birds busted out of range are not funny. But you and your hunting cronies have some responsibility to the dog, too. I've hunted young dogs with people who amble along as though they are going to a funeral. Working behind a flushing dog will give you the best possible, sporty shooting. But you have to stay up as best you can with the dog. This is not a pointing dog who will hold a bird for a week waiting for the guns to come up and get into position. You, as the dog handler, have to move the people into position. Give the dog a break. You don't want him to flush birds only to have them fly off.

The pup is going to get bolder and bolder as he gets to like the game. Once he is bold, you must control him. He should be shaken up if he decides he knows best. That's where the early training on the COME command pays off. Show me a dog that is put on a check-cord to keep him under control and

I'll show you a dog that pays no attention and does not know the COME command. For the upland hunter, COME is the ball game.

As each of you gets to know what the other wants, you will give the COME AROUND command and only make a gesturing movement in that direction. What you are hoping for is the voice turning him, after which the hand signal takes over to show him the new direction. He will get to a point where he will check back to see where you are . . . that's what we eventually want.

The diagram shows the path (dotted line) the dog will learn to take on his own while quartering a field. The solid line shows the hunter's eventual path through a field. The hunter's final path is a curve because he will indicate to the dog, by moving a few steps in the new direction, the way he wants the dog to go at the end of each side cast. At first the trainer walks the full zigzag. As the dog learns what is wanted, the trainer does a shorter zig and zag. This is the first picture of the zigzag sequence. Turn the page for the rest.

1. Start out in the middle of a field as in the first picture/diagram. You walk the zig to the edge of the field. Turn and zag to the other edge.

2. Walk in the new direction. You must constantly chatter to the dog to keep going. If he gets too far in front or to the side, call him back.

3. When you get to an edge, give the command COME AROUND and use the correct arm signal—a sweeping motion using the arm in the new direction. The dog won't know until later why he has to do all this.

1. Command SIT, one blast on the whistle.

2. A pigeon is thrown and a blank fired. The dog stays put.

3. The dog must remain steady. The bird is marked down.

4. The dog is sent on two whistles to make the retrieve.

MAKE 'EM BIRDY IN THE FIELD

This is a very exciting thing for a young dog. If he breaks, don't be too hard on him yet. Try to make him stay but also let him enjoy this. The flight of the bird is a whole new thing for Tar. To control the bird's flight, pull some of the flight feathers on one of the bird's wings. He'll fly only 40 yards.

MAKE 'EM OBEY WHISTLE FROM DISTANCE

Stand a distance behind the dog. A live bird is thrown and is shot. The dog holds. . . .

. . . Tar's head drops. He's ready to charge, but he waits for the two blasts from the whistle.

This should not be tried until you are sure that you have the necessary control in the work shown on the preceding page. If the dog is steady, you can proceed. What we are working toward is to teach him to stop on flush. Of course he won't grasp that yet. In this fun game we are teaching him that the whistle gives the commands, no matter how tempting things look.

1. Stand on the side between the dog and the shooter. Command SIT, one blast. Fly bird, shoot.

2. Two blasts send the dog. Immediately blast once for him to stop. Tar didn't!

GET 'EM READY TO STOP ON FLUSH

What we are doing here is setting the stage for upland flushing. Tar has been shown how to quarter the field. He has been made birdy. This is the next step in the control for flushing. When he flushes the bird, we want him to stop as soon as the bird is airborne. There are two reasons: First, it's a safety measure for the dog. In heavy cover a gunner may not see the dog chasing the bird. The dog could lunge up to grab the bird in the air just as the shot is fired. The other reason is that a sitting dog can mark a bird down better than a running dog.

3. Intercept him. Holler NO!

4. Give him what for, for not obeying the whistle.

SOME REFINEMENTS

GET IN . . . GET IN is used when you are close to the dog and you spot a good piece of cover. This is the command that should alert him to get in and search it out. As you give the command, point to the place you want him to go in, and when he does start in, command HUNT 'EM UP . . . HUNT 'EM UP to encourage him on. To teach him just what you mean by the GET IN command . . . go in with him. Show him that's what you want. I only wish there were a way for you to show him the command HUNT 'EM UP! But it is not dignified for you to be on all fours.

Command GET IN, GET IN. There might be a bird in there.

Point the way and go in with him.

Go in with him. Tell him to HUNT 'EM UP. That shows him what the command means.

1. He stays in close. Fifteen yards is good, or the whistle brings him back. He quarters to the right.

2. COME AROUND. He follows the hand signal for the new direction, working as he goes.

3. Tar has made game. The flush. The gunner will not shoot unless Tar responds to the single blast.

4. Tar sits ... we shoot. Tar holds until the whistle releases him. Not bad for only fifteen months old!

Hit the whistle ... shoot ... release him when the bird is down. I'm hoping he'll get the idea and do this without the STOP whistle command. With a young dog, keep the chatter going so he constantly knows you are there and in control of the situation. Stop the noise as he learns his job.

A GOOD TRAINING GAME

This game can be played at any time of the year. I take a few pigeons, shackle them, and put them out in a field, then I put the dog through the whole zigzag game. You will be so pleased when the dog discovers that there is more to these early walks than he thought. Tie a piece of rag on a bush near where you planted the birds. Work the dog into the wind and see just how far away he gets the first scent. He "makes game" by showing the excitement caused by the smells. Every part of the dog will come alive. He will wheel around, the tail will go like sixty—or I guess that should now be fifty-five. You will know when he first discovers the game! A few pigeons will last a whole training season. We had two that did their job well, so when hunting season closed we released them. For over a year they returned every night to be fed. They became part of the family. We named them Henry and Mary—don't ask me why.

You will have started the upland work more as fun and games for the pup when he is twenty weeks old, but those games become part of his basic hunting work. He will do the zigzag before he even knows what it is for, or that there is even such a thing as game birds sitting out there waiting to be found. Retrievers are naturals for this work. Except for the Chessie, who started out as a water retriever, Labs, Goldens, and Flat-Coats were used on upland game for more than a hundred years before they were used as water dogs. By the time your pup is about ten months old, he will be doing a fine job as an upland hunter. Start your pup early and you will have it made.

Chapter 7

Handling . . . Separates the Men from the Boys

HANDLING FOR BLIND RETRIEVES

Handling is what the field trialer can teach the hunter. The most exciting part of a trial is to watch a dog being "handled" to a blind retrieve. The handler knows exactly where the bird is, the dog does not . . . thus the name *blind* or *blind retrieve*. The dog is sent from the handler's side and must go straight, be it first over rough terrain, through a swamp, angle into water, and still swim the line to the bird. Judges set up the "meanest" kinds of tests you could imagine to try to make it tough on the dog. They don't usually succeed. If the dog goes straight to the bird (called *lining the bird*), some 200 yards away, he gets a perfect score. If he deviates he must be stopped by whistle. The dog stops on a dime, turns facing the handler, and receives his

The field trialer can teach the hunter much about handling. One of the top professional trainers, Bachman Doar, gives one of his dogs a line to run to "Philadelphia" and a direction to the right.

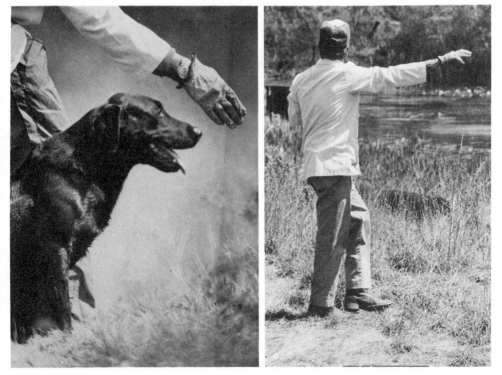

Dave Elliot at one of the first trials he ran in the United States, in 1934. He "invented" American handling.

correction by arm (hand signal). The dog will follow the signal and can be set on a handkerchief, any place, in any direction just as long as the dog is in sight of the handler. With some modification this is what every waterfowler's dog should be able to do. Marking the single fall and handling is the real ball game for the hunter.

We can take a page from the field trialer's book, but not the whole page. Some of the distances are so great that the trialer wears a white jacket so his dog can see him. How much of a daily bag do you think you would get standing in a prominent place, wearing a white jacket? Duck hunters do just the opposite: you hide and wear camouflage. These distances get to be ridiculous for the hunter, but are necessary for the trialer because the trial dog is so good that long, complicated blinds are needed to find a winner.

HOW HANDLING CAME ABOUT

The story of how handling got started in this country makes it plain why handling is so important. Dogs were not handled with whistle and hand signals in England where field trials were started, and we patterned our dog work after theirs. In the early 1930s, when field trials were started in America, a Scottish gamekeeper named Dave Elliot was brought to this country. He knew the work of the English sheep dogs, and he believed that it would be useful to apply similar methods to retrieving dogs as used with sheep dogs. He trained his retrievers to respond to whistle and hand signals. The dogs were then working under his control, and the decisions were made by him . . . not by the dogs. The judges in those early field trials had never seen dog work of this kind. They didn't know how to evaluate what they were seeing and decided that Dave was not following the rules. Poor Dave and his dogs either were not placed in the events or were thrown out!

In those days, of course, there were no rules covering handling . . . nobody knew what it was. Dave changed all of that. A dog of his became the hero of the day and proved the merit of his method. The test was a double retrieve in water. A boat was anchored about 150 yards offshore in a great, open bay. The first duck was thrown and shot from it. From another boat not far offshore a second bird was thrown and shot to fall into the decoys, 20 yards in front of the hunter's blind. The dogs, seeing all the action through a cutout in the blind, were sent to make both retrieves.

The first dog that worked showed Dave what the problem was. That dog, and those that followed, did the obvious thing: they swam out into the decoys and retrieved the second bird, brought it back to the handler, then went for the first bird out in the bay. (Left to his own devices a dog will practically always retrieve the last bird down first.) But out in the bay the current was strong, and by the time the dogs made the first short retrieve the far bird had been swept away. By the time the dog got to the place where they marked the long bird down, the bird was long gone. The dogs, *not* being trained to handle, but to go out and not return without a bird, caused great embarrassment. They would not come back, after circling around in the cold water, empty-handed, or is it empty-mouthed?

Dave brought his dog to line and decided to take a chance with the judges. The birds were shot and his dog was sent into the decoys to pick up the close bird. Then Dave stopped his dog before he reached the duck and gave him the signal to swim away from that bird and go back toward the far bird. The dog swam through the decoys, ignoring the dead duck . . . he took Dave's signal. Out in the open water his dog could see the far duck floating off and caught up with the bird before it hit the fast current. After that, the short retrieve was apple pie . . . that duck wasn't going anywhere.

That seemed to clinch the deal for Dave, and handling became the way for the retrievers. When Dave, now a very old man, told me the story, he recalled that one hard-going dog, to the horror of the gallery, swam out of sight. Another thing Dave said was that he was not very happy about handling in trials . . . he felt it is being overdone today.

What Dave did with his dog is actually "at the end of the semester," as my old chemistry professor would say. To call a dog off a bird and direct him to another, be it a mark or a blind, is the sophistication we shall work toward.

HANDLING . . . FIELD TRIALS *VERSUS* HUNTING

The retriever's job is conservation. Without dogs many birds would never be recovered. Cripples have to be retrieved before they get out of range and die. Often this has to be done at the direction of the handler. A dog must be able to take a line in the direction in which he is sent, accept corrections, and then, once in the area, use his nose to find the bird. For the hunter it is very important that the dog work be done as quickly as possible . . . get the dog back in the blind . . . get ready for the next flights of birds coming to stool . . . shooting is the important thing, not dog work. The hunter is not interested in seeing if his dog remembered the second or third fall. If the dog is not on mark, the hunter will want to correct him . . . handle him. That's the job that separates the knotheads from the hunting retrievers.

The three accompanying diagrams will explain and clarify what the hunter does and does not need from his dog and show how far away field trials have gotten from actual hunting.

Diagram 1 demonstrates the field trialer's needs. The dog comes to line (the use of a blind to conceal the hunter is eliminated . . . the bird is hidden before the dog comes to the line). The dog is sent from the line and takes a direct line across the land and into the water to the area of the hidden bird. A dog's natural instinct is to dive into the water as you do, by squaring off as you would dive into a swimming pool—but not the field-trial dog. If the handler's direction signal is to go into the water at a 20-degree angle, that is what he must do. The dog is trained to take the "line" all the way to "Philadelphia" without deviating. If he gets off course as much as about 15 degrees, the handler will stop him and move him with whistle and hand signals back onto the original course—knowing that is what the judge wants to see. The line must be as straight as possible. The judge will tell the handler before he starts his dog that the dog may not set foot on the point of land that juts out into the water (see diagram). The dog must carry out the whole task by water. Of course it is understood that the dog will go through the decoys and ignore them. When the dog has gone the distance and found the bird hidden in the tules, he must reverse his course and return the full distance by water. This test, which is rather simple for a trial dog, requires the ultimate in obedience.

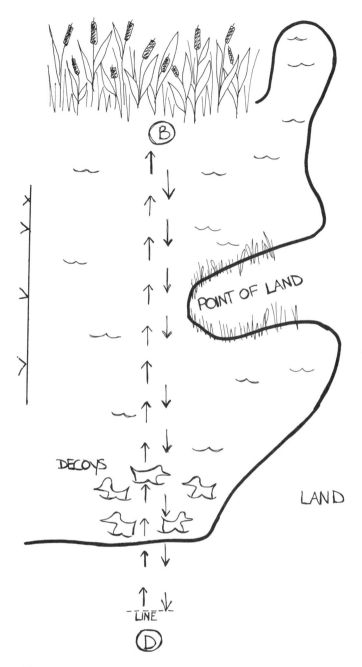

B

POINT OF LAND

DECOYS

LAND

LINE

D

Diagram 1.

Diagram 2 shows the same situation, but now it is the hunter's turn. Instead of the line to start from, a blind is used and the bird has been shot and is down out by the patch of tules at point B in the diagram. Instead of a water entry on an angle, the dog is sent on a line that will take him along the bank of the water. This "running the bank" is a no-no in the field-trial game. When the dog gets to point S, opposite where the bird has fallen, he is stopped by whistle. He is given a signal to go to the left, enter the water, and swim along the bank until his nose gets the bird's scent. When the dog picks up the bird he heads back for the land—which is natural—and runs the bank back to make the delivery. This is all accomplished in less than a quarter of the time it takes the field-trial dog to swim the distance. The hunter has his downed bird and can get back to the business at hand, which is to be ready for more birds to come in. No duck in his right mind is going to come near the decoys if some guy is out there waving his arms and whistling at a dog.

To handle a dog he must be in sight . . . if you can't see him you can't handle him. That is why the hunter did not have the dog run all the way around the edge of the water to the bird in diagram 2. If the dog had gotten into the reeds and could not be seen, the hunter would have had to give the whistle trill to command COME. Once he saw his dog again he would stop him and give the signal over to the left. All that is time-consuming, a hunter's no-no.

It is obvious from this example that the trialer's dog does a more precise job. But don't think for a moment that the hunter doesn't need precise control. In diagram 3 the hunter's situation has changed. The right-hand bank is all covered with tules and so is the land on both sides of the channel. The bird has fallen in the channel and has drifted to the left bank. The dog cannot go by land. It would be nice to have the dog take a line across the water and right down the center of the channel as a field-trial dog would do. That takes *a lot of work*—it looks good, but it's not necessary for the hunter to put that much time into the training. It will take a little more handling to get the hunter's dog to perform this test, but he'll get the job done. The diagram shows two ways the dog may go. He may swim along the bank and get into the channel, but more likely it would be in the general direction of the other path. The dog would take a general line to the area. He would be allowed to swim off course to get distance toward the fall. He would be stopped at point X and given a signal to get over to the right. When he lined up with the true course to the bird, Y, he would be stopped again and signaled to go back toward the channel. It might take some more "hacking" to get the dog to Z.

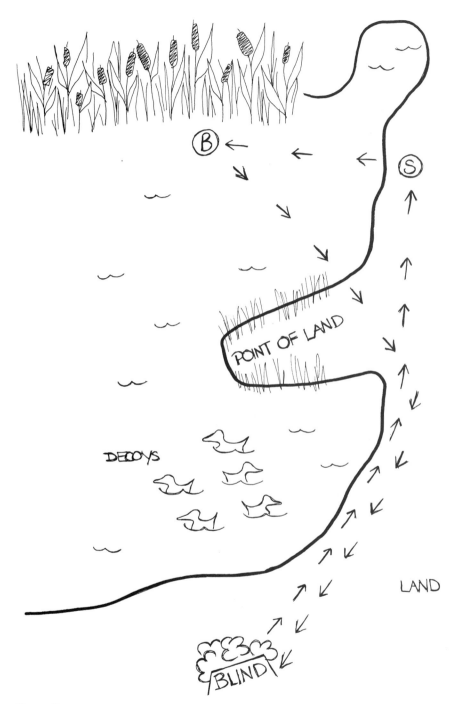

Diagram 2.

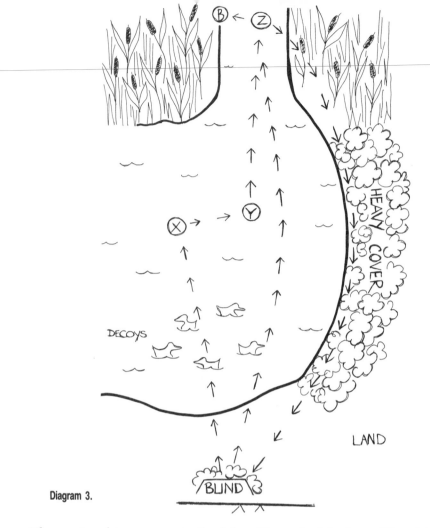

Diagram 3.

Then a signal to go over to the left will get the job done. The object for the hunter is to get the "meat." In tough situations, as in diagram 3, the hunter will have to put up with a few extra commands to the job done, but the hours of work and the assistance needed to train for clean channel blinds might not be worth it for the hunter.

Many hunters have never seen a dog handled to a downed bird and yet they have been around waterfowl and dogs for years. This is the point in training a retriever where hunters throw up their hands and say they just couldn't teach a dog to handle. Most say that they don't need all that stuff. What they are really saying is that they don't know how to go about it. I've heard all the excuses in the book. But it is not hard to teach a dog to handle. If you can teach the dog to SIT, STAY, COME . . . Tar and I will teach you how to have your dog doing simple handling work by the time he is six months old.

FOR THE RECORD

Tradition, as we have seen, often gets in the way of learning and even progress. When it comes to teaching handling, the "old wife" gets in the act again. This time the field trialer is the perpetrator. A big part of his game is to teach a young dog to mark multiple falls and develop memory. For the first two years of a field-trial dog's life he is drilled on marked falls. The game they play is that for those first two years a dog runs in the Derby stake, and that stake is made up of marked falls only. Somehow many trainers and writers on training have figured out that a dog under two years is too young to learn handling. Then the trialers have another tale. Trialers feel that if handling is taught very young the dog will become too dependent on the handler and will *pop*. This means that the dog will stop and look back to the handler for help on a tough retrieve. This is a serious no-no in trials. The Derby dog has to do it all on his own . . . the handler has to put his hands and whistle in his pocket.

The gentlemanly way to say it is that I do not subscribe to that thinking. What I should say is that for the hunter it is rubbish. First, as you will see, Tar learned the rudiments of handling while he was just a frolicking puppy. And second, with the hundred or more retrieves he has made, as I write this on his first birthday, I have still to see him pop. No way . . . he's a retrieving maniac. But if he did pop, for a hunting dog I see nothing seriously wrong with that. I like to have a hunting dog believe in me. If something goes wrong and he knows it, I see nothing wrong in giving a dog a hand signal to get the job done faster. I'd be glad to give a young dog help, because for the hunter popping is not the serious fault the trialer makes it out to be. I can add to that by saying, to his credit on this night of his first year, Tar has made some rather impressive blind retrieves—and that is the bottom line.

Here is a tip, for what it is worth, for the field trialer. If he only yard-trained for handling, and taught the young dog what the signals meant, but never used them in the field until the dog was two, the argument about handling making the dog pop would not be valid, since the dog would never know what the yard game was for. But at the same time the trainer would be ahead of the game, by teaching this when the dog was most capable of learning. Remember the Swedish baby!

A few paragraphs back I emphasized that it is easy to teach a dog to handle. Try it and if I am wrong throw the book in the garbage and call me names, but then call Tar a genius because at twenty-two weeks he had already learned the first part of the game. Call me a bum . . . but only after you have given it a go.

BASEBALL STARTS AT TWENTY WEEKS

Here is how we taught Tar, and it will be the same for your dog. The pup is twenty weeks old and will sit and stay. Right? He's been doing it by whistle for half his life. Remember we said this was the most important command for the waterfowl dog? Now we shall start to put it to use. We'll set up an imaginary baseball diamond. We walk the pup to the pitcher's mound and sit him down facing home plate by whistle. We tell him to STAY, then walk back to home plate. Command STAY and throw a dummy to first base. If he knows the command he will stay—Tar did from the first. If the pup forgets and runs to get the dummy, rush out and stop him. Take him back to the pitcher's mound and repeat STAY. Don't be rough or use an angry tone . . . just firm. Start over. If he does not stay the second time you have to realize that you two have not done your homework. The dog at this age should stay when told to. If it is not working, it is not the dog's fault . . . get back to more yard training on SIT, STAY, COME.

If you have followed us so far, from page 1 on, I can guarantee the pup will sit while the dummy is being thrown to first base. Now you are at the catcher's position and the pup on the mound. Throw the dummy to first base after commanding STAY. He'll watch it go. Wait until he looks back at you. When he does, extend your arm to the right, and at the same time give two blasts on the whistle. Step off with your right foot. Your arm movement, your whole body, is showing him the direction you want him to go. Encourage him with a rousing "Fetch it up." He'll go pick it up and bring it to you. Wipe the perspiration off your brow and praise him for all you are worth. Do it again and again. Tar got the hang of what I wanted within minutes. I kept this little game going with him until I was sure that he was sure. Next, the game is played to third base. That makes no real difference—it's the same game played on the other side—the left arm is used and your body action is to that side. I like the dog to sit and watch the dummy land, but do not send him until he has looked back for the command to go and sees all the nonsense you are doing. He'll get the idea and look to you for the signal to go. That is what we want him to learn first. As we continue this we hope he learns to associate the arm signal with the direction. Do this for a week. Do it about six times per lesson and tell him how good he is . . . because that is not bad for a twenty-week-old pup.

Through all of this you are taking him to the pitcher's mound and sitting him there, then walking to home plate and throwing to first or third. When you think he has that, throw the dummy over his head to second base. He may roll off the mound watching it go. If he breaks be ready with the one whistle blast to stop him. Go out and start over. When he gets your drift and is waiting, give the command to go back toward second base as soon as he looks back at you for directions. Here is the way the back command is given. Hold your hand straight up over your head. Wag your hand so he really sees this new position. To make him go bring your hand down to your head by bending your elbow, then throw it straight up again in the extended position—reach high—and at the same time give two blasts on the whistle to GO.

Tar had this within days, and there is no reason why a week of it will not get the idea of what you want firmly into your dog's noggin.

We are going to start baseball. This is a very important picture. Tar is now twenty weeks old. He is sure on his simple commands, and that is the name of the game at this point. You cannot start baseball until the dog will sit and let you throw out the dummies and then wait to go on command. It's a must.

Very few hunting dogs handle. Hunters seem to have such a hard time teaching handling that we are going to show it so slowly, step by step, that even my Uncle Louie could learn it. We shall start with one dummy at a time. A dummy is thrown to first base. Tar watches it go. He sees it sitting there, goes to fetch it only after he hears the two whistle blasts meaning GO. He has my direction signal to follow . . . but goodness, there is no other way to go, because only that one dummy is out there.

144

Now to the left. One dummy to third base. He already know what I'm going to do, but he waits for me.

Singals are exaggerated. I want to get it through his noggin what my arm means standing out there.

Then I send him. My body moves the way I want him to go ... there is no other choice for him.

BACK is easy. For weeks we have been playing a game with Tar. I throw a dummy, send him from my side, and make him stop by whistle on the way. Actually that places him on the pitcher's mound. When I give the hand signal to go on and fetch it up, I am using the baseball signal for BACK. For some reason trainers have problems teaching BACK. Tar learned it before he ever knew about baseball.

He knows which way to go. He is looking back over his shoulder. As you progress here, watch the dog and see where he is looking. If he looks in the wrong direction, wait and repeat your signal until you know he will respond as you want him to do.

SIT, STAY . . . AND A NEW GAME

Now you can see why the basic commands are so important. You cannot teach baseball until the dog knows SIT, STAY—no matter what his age. He also has to love to fetch. You will only be fighting the wind trying to teach this game to a dog that won't stay while you are setting the game up. Here we are only working with 20-foot retrieves, but the necessary control will be the same if it is 200 yards.

Remember, when the pup was back in first grade we started to test him at mealtime to see if he really knew to stop and sit when he heard that one blast of the whistle. Then later we did it on sitting at heel . . . blew once, threw the dummy, and he'd wait until he got the two blasts to go. If, for fun, I gave him the hand signal to go to make the retrieve and only one blast of the whistle . . . he would not go. He was that sure of what the whistle blasts meant. You might say we were teaching the dog to count. He would start to move on one blast, but not get off his tail if the second blast did not follow instantly. He was like a spring that started but didn't uncoil.

Actually we had more in mind than just a game that was fun to show off to friends. Before Tar was twenty weeks old we extended that test to include stopping on whistle when he was about halfway to the dummy. When the pup was sent to retrieve a dummy and stopped, he was then given the GO BACK command to have him go on to make the retrieve . . . two whistles, arm motion over the head and all. He did it naturally because he wanted the dummy. He didn't know or care yet what the hand signal was for—he just heard the releasing GO command. I could have stood on my head and he would have learned by association that that meant to go back and get the dummy. When we started to play baseball at twenty weeks, he was already unconsciously learning the hand signal to GO BACK. The reason I started this fun game early with him was that trainers seem to have more trouble teaching going back to second base than to first or third.

As soon as I was sure he would stop on whistle without fail on land, I started it in water . . . something he would be required to do later in life. But I did not, repeat, *did not* do this in water until I was absolutely sure he would obey, since correcting him would have been a problem. Never let yourself get into a position where you cannot enforce your command (that's called getting into a box).

Some might say that interrupting the retrieve with a young dog will dampen the dog's enthusiasm to retrieve. Garbage—if you have made him crazy to retrieve . . . nothing will dampen him.

We started all these yard games at twenty weeks, without expecting too much, and continued them as the weeks went on. It was amazing how quickly Tar caught on to things. By the time he was six months old he could be moved a yard at a time . . . or as fast as the whistle commands could be given. I could send him to make the retrieve of a dummy and stop him ten

All through the book I've been saying how important SIT, STAY, COME are. This series show just what . . .

Dog is sent . . .   . . . stopped . . .   . . . sent on . . .   . . . stopped . . .   . . . brought back .

THE REAL MEANING OF SIT, STAY, COME

times, or as often as I wished. I could stop him and make him sit a yard from the dummy, then give him the trill, COME IN command, and he would come toward me without picking up the dummy. Then I would stop him and send him back for it. That's the kind of control we are working for. That is the real meaning of SIT, STAY, COME.

... I mean by those commands. They are as precise as clockwork under all conditions, with no excuses.

... sent on ...   ... stopped ...   ... sent on, stopped ...   ... stopped before pickup.

HAND SIGNALS . . . MAKE THEM CLEAR . . . EXAGGERATE

Hunters must use different signals from the field trialer. The hunter is often dressed in dark clothes. He has to be seen by the dog against all kinds of backgrounds. Make sure the dog is looking at you. Put your arm out and show the dog what you want. Pull your arm back when you feel he sees you and understands. Throw your arm out and blast twice for him to move OVER (top). For BACK (bottom) the arm goes up to be clearly seen, down, then up again, like a pump, to send him. Help the dog, exaggerate the signals.

Many hunters give the BACK signal as if trying to push the dog away from them. The pictures show how little the dog sees when the hunter is camouflaged and the hand is against the body.

The hand signal for the dog to take a line is precise. The hand is held above his head, between his eyes, and points the way. The motion to send him is a slight forearm and wrist movement forward.

The next step is to teach the STOP control in water. We make sure he knows what he is doing on land . . .

Do the same thing in water. You'd better be sure the dog knows what he is doing, because you have no way . .

. . . Throw the dummy. Send him. Stop him by whistle. Then send him on to make the retrieve.

. . . of getting out to him and making the correction. If you have done your homework, he'll do it.

START PUTTING IT ALL TOGETHER

So far we have been playing baseball with only one dummy. We have hoped that with the one dummy, and therefore with only one way to go to pick it up, Tar, the little sponge, would have learned to associate the exaggerated hand signals with the direction we wanted him to go in. After a few days, or take a week if you want, a second dummy was introduced. We used the same setup: walked him to the pitcher's mound, went to home plate and then threw to first and third, in that order. Now we are going to help the pup . . . remember, a retriever will naturally go to the last bird down. That is third base—that is the one we send him for first. Take him back to the pitcher's mound, and when you are back at home plate, send him to first base for the other retrieve. By the second day of this he will have it down as easily as Uncle Louie could put down a beer. Then take him the next step: this time, when you set him up and throw the second dummy to third base, try to fool him and send him for first base instead. I'll bet Uncle Louie's beer mug that your pup will do it . . . now he is *really* following your hand signal. There is a choice out there and he took the one you wanted, which was against his natural instinct.

A week of this and he will be sure. Then do the same thing, using first and second base, and throwing to second base last. What is your guess as to how he will do? One thing to be careful of . . . when he does this don't pop the buttons off your shirt.

Don't expect a flawless job and don't lose your temper even when you think he should be perfect; make this a fun game. In a week or even less add a third dummy. Start the same way and send him for the last dummy down. Then load the bases and take your choice. In a short time he will get good at all this. Start to fool him if you can—if he seems to have his mouth watering for a special one of the three, send him for another. If he is sitting crooked on the mound, send him for a dummy where he has to turn around to get it . . . you will know then if he understands. Of course this is just the beginning, but this is the basis of the work, as a duck hunter's dog, that he will do the rest of his hunting life. All this will be expanded from a living-room-size baseball diamond to one that will extend as far as "Philadelphia."

I have a friend who actually did train a dog to play baseball in his living room, using three gloves, during the bad months of the winter, and in the spring the pup did 100-yard blind retrieves . . . with style.

If you are still a doubter and do not believe what a young dog can learn, look at these pictures. Here is a sixteen-week-old pup playing the complete game of baseball. He is taken to the pitcher's mound and told to SIT and STAY. Then the game was set up while the pup waited. He followed every hand signal without fault.

Let me reassure you of something. Suggest to an old-line trainer that a five-month-old pup can start his handling lessons, and that will prompt a lecture on pushing the pup too fast. There is no hard evidence that this is so. What we are doing and what he is saying are two different things. We are not pushing . . . we are bringing the pup along at his own pace. Let's go to the next step.

BASEBALL . . . BIG-LEAGUE STUFF

1. Start this game as soon as he has done all the parts separately—OVERs and BACKs.

2. At first walk him to the pitcher's mound each time he makes a retrieve. Throw into the empty spot.

3. If he makes a mistake, stop him with the whistle. Walk out and take him back to the pitcher's mound.

4. Start over. If he knows, but goofs, tell him he's stupid and to pay more attention to you.

5. Now start the game from home plate. Once he knows to "line," send him to the pitcher's mound.

6. Tar did all this at about thirty weeks. Try it: you'll be surprised at how fast they learn to play ball.

LINE . . . TO PHILADELPHIA

We have been playing baseball by walking the pup to the pitcher's mound. Now we are both going to start at home plate. The pup is brought to heel and sat by whistle. From the very beginning, every time he was sent for a retrieve we did it by using the hand in front of his head to show him the way—even if it was being done on a lawn and he could see the dummy. Now, sitting at home plate, there is nothing out there in front of him . . . no dummies. Send the pup toward second base, using the hand, and move him out with the two blasts of the whistle. He should go. If that confuses him, start over. Send him out again. If he still does not get your drift, send him again, and this time as he starts to move, throw a dummy in front of him—5 yards or so. Keep repeating this until he gets the idea that he is to move out . . . and if he does, something good will be out there for him. He'll start to believe you soon and that will pay off in dividends later. It's the old game: Trust me, do what I want, and you will get what you want.

Once you have him going out as far as the pitcher's mound, 10 or 15 yards, stop him with the whistle. Once sitting, he will turn to see what this is all about. That is when you throw out the dummies to first, second, and third bases and start to play baseball. From then on, when you play the game you no longer walk him out to the pitcher's mound—he will be sent. He will soon get the idea that the hand at his head that sends him directs him.

You might say that this is the beginning of taking a line out to nowhere. There are things I often do before I start the formal lesson of taking a line. I start by walking the dog down a path or woods road—we are just out for a stroll. I will drop a dummy without his seeing it and then walk on. Then I will bring him to heel and send him back for the dummy. He sees it and of course goes for it. Next time we take the same walk I will do the same thing and walk on twice the distance, then bring him to heel and send him back for it. The game goes on in the same place, getting longer and longer until the dummy is out of sight. Tar would go 100 yards down a path . . . knowing that if I sent him it would have to be there. The trick is never to fail your dog. If you send him, a dummy *must* be there!

You go to the next step when you think he is ready. I forget exactly when Tar started the line game, but it was when he was about five and a half months old. You will know when your dog is ready for this. If you have a long field with high grass, it is the best, but if not, a path or woods road will do the trick. With an ordinary lawn mower cut a path the full length of the field . . . 200 yards would be sensational, especially if the end of the path crests over a rise or hill. Take about ten dummies and you and the dog start at one end and walk down the path. As you go, drop dummies off starting at 10 yards, then at 20, then 40, and so on. The idea is to make them closer at the beginning of the run and then farther apart at the end. He sees it all and there are no tricks up your sleeve . . . almost none. Take the pup to the beginning and send him for the first dummy—he'll go because he can see the first one. When he returns, send him on farther for the second, then third, fourth, and so on. The trick is to have him run down the path without seeing the last one over the crest. The high grass or wooded path will keep him in line. There is no question that he will get them all and be moving out 200 yards before you know it. He'll learn that if you send him, even if he sees nothing at first, something good will be out there. When he has done this, turn the game around and do it from the other end of the field just so he won't get the idea the place has anything to do with what we want. Soon you can forget the short retrieves and put a whole pile of dummies at the end of the path and he'll run and bring them back one by one. Then hide the pile of dummies at the end of the path. He'll believe! At about six or seven months try this lining game in part of the field that is not mowed into a path. He will have the idea but might need some help in the unmowed field—run out and give it to him, then start over. Make them shorter retrieves in the unmowed field, then gradually increase the distances.

What about doing this in water? No problem. Throw a dummy out, then throw another farther out in the same line. When I've gotten them out

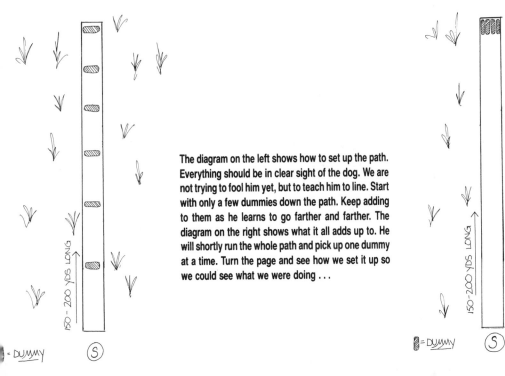

The diagram on the left shows how to set up the path. Everything should be in clear sight of the dog. We are not trying to fool him yet, but to teach him to line. Start with only a few dummies down the path. Keep adding to them as he learns to go farther and farther. The diagram on the right shows what it all adds up to. He will shortly run the whole path and pick up one dummy at a time. Turn the page and see how we set it up so we could see what we were doing . . .

150 - 200 YDS LONG

150 - 200 YDS LONG

= DUMMY

(S)

= DUMMY

(S)

1. This is easy to teach if you follow the logic of building the distances slowly.

as far as I can throw, I use a Retriev-A-Launch and shoot them out farther, in line. Then I send the dog. Tar learned this fast because we worked from a high bank and he could see the dummies all lined up like floating soldiers. The hand showed him the way. After he learned that he was to swim rather far to get the dummies we went to the next step. From the same high bank I sent him with no dummies out there in the water. When he went—made the plunge and swam in the right direction—I threw a dummy out in front of him. At first they were very short throws. This was to teach him that if he dove in and swam in the right direction he got his reward. Then the distances were increased. Soon the distance became so great that I had to use the launcher. Here, you might run into a problem. At first, without seeing any dum-

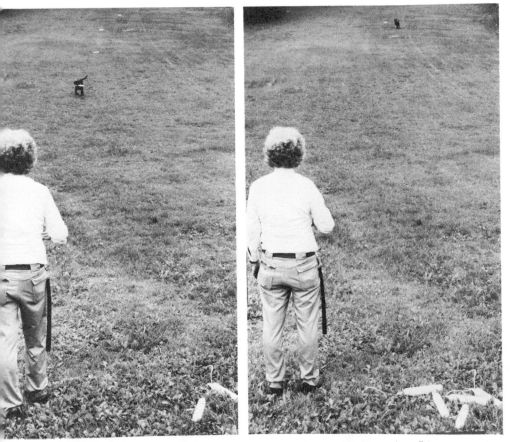

2. If the pup sees them, he'll get them. The idea is to teach him that he has to run a long distance.

mies out there to retrieve, your dog may become confused. Some dogs will turn and pop if you are not fast enough in throwing the dummy or are not anticipating how far he will go on his own. Some dogs even learn that the dummy is coming from you. If the pup pops, you have a few alternatives. If he does it only a short distance from the shore, call him back and sternly start over. If he is out a ways, and turns looking for help, ignore him . . . outstare him or even turn your back to him. He'll get the idea. But do not worry about the popping business in water because young dogs, or even older dogs learning this, often go through this phase. They'll outgrow it. Just keep going with the above plan and very shortly you will have a retriever that will go to Philadelphia, Pennsylvania, by land or sea.

DON'T NEGLECT WHAT THE DOG HAS LEARNED

Let me interrupt the procedure to remind you that while we are going ahead we are continually going back to the earlier lessons. SIT, STAY, COME are constantly being sprung on the dog . . . longer and longer singles are given . . . he's given more experience in quartering . . . water work is ex-

Here is the same path game, but it has a trick at the end. The dog is sent down the path for the dummies and he brings them back one at a time. Then he gets to a point where there are no more out there to be seen. He does not know that we have hidden one in the bushes at the end of the path. Once the ones in sight have been picked up, send him for the "blind." If he follows your directions, goes down the empty path and finds the blind, you will know that he believes in you. That is mighty important.

tended, and so on. I do not feel it is necessary to spell it all out here, but the dog is extended and given practice in everything he has learned by constant repetition as you train him in the new work. It is your responsibility as the teacher to think out each step as you go along.

Here is an example of what I mean by extending. The harder and harder lessons will be learned by rote as the dog accomplishes the tests, but things like memory have to be developed on his own, and you can help. Here is how. Shoot a long retrieve with the Retriev-A-Launch and then a very short one. Send the dog for the short one and as soon as he returns with it, do not send him by giving the direction sign with your hand in front of his head. Instead, just blow the two blasts to GO as soon as he has made the first delivery. See if he remembers where that other dummy was shot. To start this both dummies should be seen. As he gets the idea, shoot that first dummy into cover, so he has to use his head instead of his eyes. Keep in mind that the new lesson you are working on is important, but so are the past things, and keep expanding them.

LINE . . . AROUND THE CLOCK

We now have the dog moving out on a line, and the distances are rather impressive. Here is a very simple game to teach the dog that the hand shows him the way. Start with four dummies and both of you go to the pitcher's mound. With the dog at heel, throw a dummy to each of the four bases. Then set the dog up facing, say, home plate. Send him. Next turn to second base and do the same thing, then at third and first, just like going around the clock. By repetition the dog will learn the hand shows him the way. After he learns this, increase the number to eight dummies and throw them around the clock with the added dummies at 1:30, 4:30, 7:30, and 10:30 to make the work a little more precise. Field-trial dogs are trained this way and given the test with two rings of dummies—the outer ring has dummies placed between the eight in the inner ring. They then have to go past the dummies on the inner ring to pick up those in the outer, or they will be mixed up, first inner, then outer ring. That kind of precision is not needed by the hunter.

If you can get to the point of playing this game with four dummies, in cover so the dog does not see them, your dog will be getting the idea of what you want.

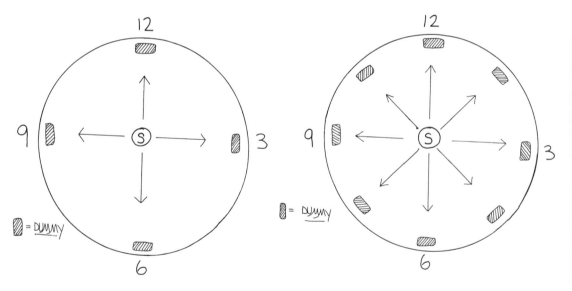

Stand at the center of the imaginary clock with your dog. Start with the left-hand, easier pattern. Throw the dummies around the clock. He sees it all. Then set him up properly and use the hand to guide him to the one you want. Once he has that, do the more complicated pattern. It shows him he is to follow that hand. Make the clock bigger and bigger.

FROM LINING PHILADELPHIA . . . EXTEND BASEBALL

To extend baseball we can use the same field, with a modification, that we did to teach line. It is simple, but it might be best to show you in a drawing. You cut paths perpendicular to the long one that was used to teach lining. It is suggested that the long path be about 100 or 150 to 200 yards and the "arms" about 30 to 40 or more yards, if you have the space on each side. The first path cut across the line should be about 40 yards from the starting line, the second one about 80 yards. If you have a path or woods road something like the configuration of the diagram, you can use that. This T or double T will help the dog understand what you want him to do by giving him paths to follow.

Your dog should be ready to do this game as soon as he is fairly dependable at playing baseball on the lawn and after he has learned to take the line on the big path. Tar was about seven months old when we started this game.

Here Tar showed off the drive and desire we developed to retrieve dummies, and this was the culmination of his ability to sit, stay, and come. To start this game we laid the dummies out on the path and Tar walked along with me and saw all the dummies go down. We are not trying to fool the dog in any sense of the word when we start. Diagram A shows how the dummies are put down.

All retrieves are made from the starting point at S. The dog has been taught the long line, so as a warm-up we send him to picking the dummy at the first cross point. Then the dog is sent down the path and stopped (one blast, SIT) at that cross point where he just picked up that first dummy. He is given the GO BACK signal (two blasts, GO) to go back for the bird at the second cross point. Now it all becomes dealer's choice. Send the dog to the first cross and stop him. Give him the command to go toward "first base." Since we laid the dummies down all along the path, on all the side arms, the dog will see the dummy he's being sent to. Send him off with the whistle command. Next try third base, stopping him first at the first cross point. Next send him down the path to the second cross . . . or would you like to have him go all the way to the end of the line to get a dummy? Then send him to the second cross. Give him a signal to go over to the side of your choice. Mix it up, stop him at the first cross, and give him a directional signal. As he "cleans up" the dummies on each arm, he is going farther and farther . . . he is learning to take longer and longer side casts.

You now will have the dog going in all directions of your choice—except

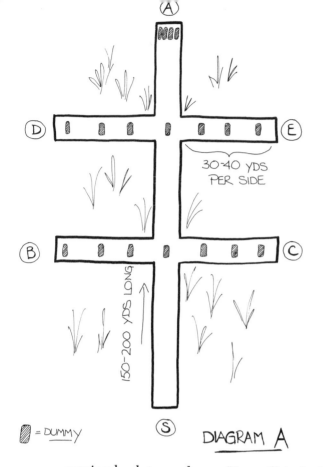

Ⓐ

Ⓓ   Ⓔ

30-40 YDS
PER SIDE

Ⓑ   Ⓒ

150-200 YDS LONG

🮤 = DUMMY   Ⓢ   DIAGRAM A

coming back toward you. You will include COME with the trill whistle in the exercise by sending him down the line and throwing a dummy onto the path behind him as he runs. He won't know it is there. Stop him and then call him in toward you. He'll think you are nuts, but if he follows the command and comes in . . . there is a dummy for him!

If he becomes a wise guy and decides to cut this all short by running out of the path (not taking your line) toward a dummy he of course knows is there, stop him, call him back, tell him NO, NO, and start over. He must follow your direction signal down the path.

Play this game until he shows that he knows what it is all about. Then you can begin setting the dummies out as shown in diagram B. Start the dog out in the new setup with the line retrieves where paths cross. Then start the poker game . . . dealer's choice . . . back all the way to the end of the run . . . out again and stop, come back toward you to find a dummy in the path . . . or back toward you and then a stop at one of the crossings, then over on one of the arms to make the retrieve. There are many combinations, mix

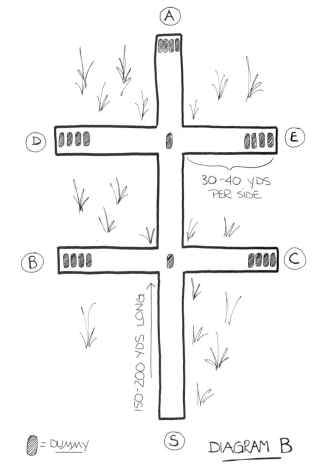

A

D   E

30-40 YDS
PER SIDE

B   C

150-200 YDS LONG

▨ = DUMMY   S   DIAGRAM B

them up . . . keep him guessing. You may find that some directions come harder than others for him—practice them. Next, if possible, hide the dummies at the end of the arms. He should be able to figure this all out, since he is playing the game of extended baseball on his home grounds.

According to the amount of time you put into this, it could be learned by his eighth or ninth month. To learn it by ten months should be a snap.

Go into a new field with no paths and set a few dummies out at each place, forming the double T. The distances should start out shorter because the dog has no paths to follow. Tie ribbons of cloth on the bushes near where you place them so you will see where they are from the line. Try to hide them with grass or leaves so the dog will not see them from a distance. Go through the same double-T procedure that we have talked about here. The obvious next step is to plant some simple blinds for the dog, using dead birds. These blinds should be short; 30 or 40 yards will do to start. Try to introduce some water into them—short swims. Over the next six months you will make them longer and longer and tougher and tougher . . . and that is handling.

1. Set the dog up. Nothing is out there. Send him on his way with the whistle.

2. If he goes in the right direction, throw the dummy ahead of him ... it's his reward.

GO IN THE RIGHT DIRECTION AND GET YOUR REWARD ...

. . . SAME THING FROM THE PITCHER'S MOUND

The next step is to do the same thing from the pitcher's mound. Give him the signal. If he takes it in spite of there being no dummy behind him, give him his reward . . . the dummy.

Casts to the side get tricky because the dog sees out of the corner of his eye that you are throwing the dummies. So he runs, then turns and looks for the throw. Solve this by having a helper carry a dummy that he cannot see. When he takes the correct cast to the side and passes the assistant, let him throw it. Fooled him!

PROBLEM? . . . DON'T BE SO SMART

Fences can be a great help. Tar is given a line . . .

. . . to the corner, stopped, and given a direction . . .

. . . over along the fence . . . doesn't have much choice . . .

. . . Back through the open gate and there is his reward.

USE WHATEVER YOU CAN TO HELP HIM UNDERSTAND

The fence can be used for dogs that run wide out of the area of fall. Shoot a dummy into a corner of a fenced-in area; the fence will hold him in. For the dog that switches on a double . . . goes to one bird, then runs to the other . . . shoot two dummies parallel to the fence, one on either side: the fence will prevent the switch. To be a good trainer you have to use your head.

Tar is set up . . .

. . . takes the line . . .

. . . starts to meander . . .

SIX MONTHS OLD . . . TAR'S VERY FIRST BLIND

. . . takes another BACK . . .

. . . scents the dummy.

Simple blind, but he did it!

... is stopped on whistle ...   ... takes a wide BACK ...   ... is stopped on the line ...

VOICE ADDED TO WHISTLE COMMANDS

The extension of the baseball into long casts to the right, left, or back will take time. The distances should gradually be increased and changes in terrain and cover should be included. The dog should get the idea that you might—and indeed will—send him anywhere to make a retrieve. Water is added to the mix, and he should be comfortable going from land to water, or from water to land, or water-land-water or land-water-land. I use the voice to help, if the dog is in a position to hear it. The voice is like bringing up the heavy artillery. When I think it is going to be a difficult cast, I will send the dog off with the two blasts of the whistle after he has seen the hand signal . . . then when he is going in the correct direction I shout after him, "BACK," or if it is a side cast, "OVER." These are traditional words used by field trialers to cast their dogs off. I use them as a reinforcement but not very often. What I am really doing is shouting at the dog, "You better get your tail going in that direction and keep going until I blow the whistle for you to stop . . . or else!"

173

Once the dog understands line, make him believe. Have a helper throw a shackled duck into the pond . . .

Line the dog up as though you were going to send him. Command NO, NO. Then reheel the dog. Face him away . . .

TRUST ME . . . YOU'LL GET YOUR REWARD

. . . the duck. Then starts to wonder if I'm nuts. He turns to make sure what this is all about. That is natural for a young dog. I then give him a BACK command and hope he believes in me . . .

. . . from the bird. Make sure you convey the new direction. Command DEAD BIRD. Send the dog. If he veers toward the duck, stop him. Call him back and start over until he understands. "Tar, DEAD BIRD!" He obeys, swims past . . .

. . . He does! Back he turns, away from the duck he can see, taking a blind line. That's when an unseen helper throws a duck out from the bushes in front of the swimming dog. Hunters often need to get a bird that is wounded before the one that is dead among the decoys. DEAD BIRD means . . . follow the hand . . . get your reward!

1. Here is a test of control and belief. Throw a dummy. He sees it. Reheel the dog; command DEAD BIRD. That's his signal that it's something else you want. Send him on a new line. Stop him, give new direction.

3. Once he is clear of the drifting dummy, stop him by whistle. Give him the new direction, which is COME IN. My hand signal shows him to stay clear of the dummy. Keep the "come-in" whistle going.

5. The whistle blows, "Come to me! Come to me!" My arms make a "come-in" motion. When he obeys, I can then stop him and give him the BACK signal and release him with the two blasts. He has swum "my pattern."

CONTROL IS WHAT IT IS ALL ABOUT

2. The dog should ignore the dummy and swim on a line behind it. He already knows that that is not what he is after. Passing that close takes real belief on his part that you will give him a reward.

4. The come-in whistle is blown hard and loud to "talk" to him, saying "Come toward me, NOW!" He can't stand it any longer and veers toward the dummy. Now he has to be obedient! The whistle becomes urgent.

6. The DEAD BIRD command is always given before a dog is sent on a blind retrieve, to alert him to what will be expected. This, the command says, is not a marked retrieve . . . follow me! Not too bad for young Tar.

SOME HANDLING REFINEMENTS

These handling refinements become dealer's choice. The hunter does not really need them, but it surely will not hurt to have them in the dog's noggin. There are many that the field trialer uses, but only two will be discussed here. The first one has to do with taking a very precise line.

Place three dummies out: one at 12:00 o'clock, one at 11:00 o'clock, and one at 1:00 o'clock. Start at about 30 feet and send the dog from heel, giving him the line to the middle one, at the 12:00 position. Then send for the 11:00 and 1:00. If he goes for the wrong one, stop him and bring him back and start again until he takes that middle one first. When he gets that done, start with one of the end ones. Mix it up until he learns to take the exact line you give him and gets the one you want. Help the dog along by setting him up slowly and really emphasizing that line with the directing hand. When that is accomplished, step back a few yards, which makes the angle narrower. Go through the procedure again . . . step back and narrow the angle . . . then step back again.

The old shell game—which cup has the pea under it? Follow the hand, get the right one. The farther back you move, the tighter the angle gets.

Set the same game up from the pitcher's mound. This will teach the dog to turn left when you use your right arm, and the reverse. To quarter back is ➤ field-trial stuff, but it comes in handy.

The other drill is to teach the dog to take the back command, but instead of going straight back, to go back on a 45-degree angle. The dog sits on the pitcher's mound and three dummies are thrown to the same positions as in the last lining drill: 11:00, 12:00, and 1:00. The arm signals will be straight over the head for the 12:00 dummy, pointing to 1:30 with the right hand for the right angle back, and pointing the arm up to the 10:30 position for left back. That means the dog will turn to his left to go back when you use your right arm, and to his right for your left. With enough training on this, you can get the dog to turn right or left and go straight back by using one or the other arm straight over your head. Of course, that gets rather sophisticated, and you won't really need it in hunting.

YOU'VE GOT A WORKING RETRIEVER

When you get your dog this far, you can take him any place and hunt any kind of birds and you will be very proud. You will have a dog that is under control and knows his job. The dog will learn your specific game of hunting just by doing it with you. Between what his parents have given him and what you have taught him, he'll be a hunter . . . a worker . . . *and that is what this book has been all about.*

Chapter 8

Testing the Hunting Retriever

THE PLIGHT OF THE HUNTER AND HIS DOG

In 1982 a group of seven hunters saw the handwriting on the wall. They met with the purpose of saving their dogs. They had seen the fate of every hunting breed that became popular in the American Kennel Club show ring ... the dogs lost their ability to hunt. That meant there were tens of thousands of puppies being sold to the public that were poorly bred for their work ... a hunter's plight.

The licensed AKC field-trial game, which has been in existence in this country for sixty-one years, cut the average hunter out of that game by sheer dollars. It is still played by only the very wealthy. There was really no place in the dog world for the hunter's retriever. He was not interested in the show ring and didn't have the money for the licensed field work. The AKC provided no other outlet.

Actually, the AKC licensed field-trial game is not the place for the hunter; it has its faults. When field-trials started in the U.S. in 1931 they were truly for the hunter. The rules, never written down, simulated hunting as it was done in Scotland. Today it is no longer a hunter's game. The error from the start was that it became an "American-type" contest, dog against dog, with the judges having to find four winners and placing them. The error, as you will see, is in the judging. It is interesting to note that the Scottish trials are also a competition of dog against dog. But that original hunting game is still played in Scottish field-trials today. To this day they do it as their grandfathers did when the game started in 1903. It is still a hunter's game for them, and judging did not become a factor and change the game.

What happened in America, with its basic competitive nature, was that the judges started making tests harder and harder to find the winners. The judging attitude soon became, OK, see if you can do *this* test! The professionals, and it has always been a professional's game, trained their dogs to do whatever the judges threw at them. So the judges, to find the winners, had to get more and more "creative." In return the dogs were trained to beat the judges. Over years of this distressing cycle, the tests got farther and farther from hunting. Today it is an exhibition of the most fantastic obedience dog work possible. The electric collar is a must in this training because the tests are no longer natural to the dog. One example: The dog is trained to not believe or use his hunting nose . . . and that makes the game useless for the hunter. AKC field-trials are played with game birds and shotguns in the field, and that is where the similarity to hunting ends.

The hunter's problem has been that he's had no place to go to find pups from hunting stock. He could not get the licensed field-trial pups for two reasons: 1. There are only about 1,000 serious people in the licensed field-trials game, and they did not produce enough pups for the big hunter market. 2. Those pups were too expensive even if he could find them. So the hunter had to get his pups from the Sunday newspaper where dogs were advertised as AKC registered . . . which means nothing as far as hunting ability is concerned.

All this time the retrievers were becoming very popular in the show ring. The show breeding for a pet market bred the work out of the dogs. By 1992 the Labrador had "earned" the title as the most popular dog in America . . . that could have spelled disaster as it did for the cocker spaniel, AKC English setter, the poodle, Irish setter, and the list goes on of the dogs ruined for the field. But now for the first time a dog with that *unfortunate title of the most popular* has been saved, and there are now puppies from hunting stock for any hunter.

NAHRA COMES TO THE RESCUE

Those seven hunters that got together ten years ago saw this popularity contest coming. The show ring was a beauty pageant with no concern for the animal's natural ability, which took centuries of breeding to acquire. Yearly statistics showed the trend. The Labrador's numbers were exploding. Just in time, the seven hunters started an organization called the North American Hunting Retriever Association. Their purpose was to test dogs for their hunting ability. Those dogs that showed they were truly hunters would be recorded for a gene pool of hunting stock. NAHRA has had more than 80,000 entries in the testing program over the last ten years. They run more than 100 events a year and have about 8,000 members in NAHRA clubs. They got what they wanted. Now, ten years later, there is a printed NAHRA Working Stud Book. It is the only *working dog* stud book in the world. The stud books of all

The walk-up . . . an upland test.

other organizations that register dogs list every pup that comes down the pike, and have nothing to do with working ability. This working stud book lists only dogs that have completed and passed field tests that simulate real hunting situations. The seven hunters made a written standard for the exact work that a hunting dog should perform. NAHRA divides the dogs into four classes, Beginner, Started, Intermediate, and Senior. The Beginner can earn a certificate, but all the others earn a title to be placed on the dog's pedigree.

Clubs were formed from coast to coast and in Alaska, Canada, and Mexico. Hunters had to be taught to train their dogs and judges taught how to do the testing. It has become an enjoyable game but with a most important purpose.

In spite of what the AKC licensed field-trials became, they had a most important service for our retrievers. While the show ring was systematically taking the work out of the retrievers to supply the pet market, the licensed field-trialers, in spite of their small numbers, kept the work in the breeds. They have been breeding some of the best retrievers in the world. When NAHRA started, they were the beginning point for breeding. Puppies from these dogs were trained as hunters, and with their new NAHRA titles make up today's hunter's stock. Now after generations of NAHRA titles, professionals and serious breeders are producing fine animals. What started as a few is now many-fold.

NAHRA has grown into a national organization. If you put a pin in a map of the United States showing where each club is located, you will see that they almost duplicate our four waterfowl flyways. What the organization has done for the dogs and the hunter is remarkable. The hunter has come out of the woodwork to get into this act. Ten years ago the hunter and his dog needed a lot of help. Neither knew their job or how to go about learning it. Very few could do the work that most of the dogs are doing today. They have learned! The NAHRA dog work today is astonishing! They do triple retrieves on water and land . . . can handle blind retrieves with uncanny control . . . quarter a field better than a springer spaniel and sit on flush, and make the retrieve on command . . . trail wounded birds like a bloodhound . . . and work from a boat or a blind. They will do all this with manners of a well-behaved child. It's impressive; they do their work with fine style. NAHRA dogs have taken their place as important conservationists. The basic NAHRA rules and concept will never change.

New businesses have evolved. NAHRA members interested in breeding a line of hunting dogs have become very successful. They run their breeding stock to show what they have to offer. Just about every region has a professional trainer to help with specific problems. These are NAHRA members who are most helpful with young, new clubs. The professional runs his own dogs in the NAHRA events but they are not the criteria for judging. The written standard is the criteria; it is based on real hunting situations and is directed to the hunter's needs. Running a dog against a written standard makes the training of a dog so much easier. NAHRA field tests are not

The dog handler handles the gun.

seeking placements as the AKC licensed judge must do. The judges do not try to find the best dog; they judge the dog on his hunting work. This means that dogs are not running against dogs, or to say that another way, people are not running against people. This takes competition out of the dog work. This makes it a whole different game from licensed field trials. The old joke is that as a handler walks his dog to line, another competitor, a "friend," says, "Good luck." Then under his breath he says, "I hope he breaks a leg." That attitude is gone in the NAHRA program because the judges do not care if one dog or all the dogs in an event win their points and ribbon. That means that people are willing to help people. There are no training secrets. It makes for a friendly game and a family sport.

Although the main purpose of NAHRA is to develop a gene pool of working stock and the working stud book, there is much fun for people along the way. First, to create a well-behaved working retriever is no different than a sculptor creating a statue. The artist starts with a rock and chips away with mallet and chisel until he finishes his work. That is not much different than taking a pup, a lump of fur, and step by step "chipping away" and ending with a well-controlled conservationist. That is a tremendous satisfaction ... It is *your* creation.

The fun for people is the out-of-doors and field tests in wonderful areas. The winning of a ribbon and points on a dog's title is a happy scene at the end of a trial ... they whoop it up for their dog and their fellow trainer's dog. After earning the title in the dog's category the fun is to acquire enough points to be invited to one of the eight regional events. It's a thrill even for the handler of a Started dog to go to his regional. For the Senior dog the title of Master Hunting Retriever is a proud victory. Then the excitement builds, to qualify the master with enough points to win a berth at the yearly national Invitational. Those that pass that same written standard in this impressive event become the North American Hunting Retriever Team of that year. That dog will be top drawer and fine breeding stock.

IT IS NOT A NEW IDEA

The idea for some sort of field testing for hunting dogs is not a new one. Thirty years ago the hunter was making a stab at testing his dogs. Without an organization to set the standard, however, nothing came of it. But as I write this I think back thirty years and laugh at one memorable day. Our little club of devoted hunters held an event that I guess we called a Gun Dog stake. I was asked to judge the event with *Field and Stream*'s humorist-writer Ed Zern, of "Exit Laughing" fame. Ed and I built a duck blind out of anything we could find and covered it with bushes. The handler and his dog had to sit in the blind. That was fine. When the birds were released, the handler was to stand up and shoot a popper (a blank). That, too, was fine. Then we called for the marshal to bring a tub of water for the handler to stand in. That was not fine. The committee gave us a questioning stare but produced the tub. Ed, seeing their concern, simply stated casually that he *always* hunted ducks with wet feet. We got away with that . . . but when we insisted that the field-trial committee produce a flower-sprinkling can so we could pour water over the handler as he sat with his dog, saying we always hunted in the rain . . . that was less than fine! The committee threatened to banish us from the field—then did . . . and that was very fine. Ed and I went to a bar and ruminated about the good old days when hunters were the backbone of America, made it strong, and the bluebird weather was for those sissy golfers.

A TYPICAL UPLAND GUN DOG TEST

Here is a typical hunting situation in which the retriever is used as an upland dog. It has been forty-five or fifty years since this kind of test has been run, yet my guess is that half the hunting retrievers in the country are used on upland game. The field (see diagram), knee-high in cover, is a typical one for pheasant or quail. It is bordered by a road on one side and very heavy cover on the other. The hunter, carrying a gun, starts with his dog 200 or more feet downwind of the planted game. The dog is cast off. He has to sweep the field and cover as much of it as possible, just like a Springer. When the handler, who walks a straight line, approaches the end of the course, the gun walks in toward the bird. When the dog gets a whiff of bird scent, makes game, and zeros in on the bird, a boy hidden behind a hill pulls a string that releases the bird. The gunner fires and drops the bird. As this is happening the handler must shoulder his empty gun as if he were actually hunting. The handler commands his dog to stop and SIT. The dog is then released to make the retrieve and delivery to hand . . . a lot of action in a few split seconds!

Dogs score high if they check out the area that has the bird scent, then move on. The judges look for the dog that comes around when ordered to do so. Control is an important part of the upland work. The judges look for the dog that moves well and seems to enjoy his work.

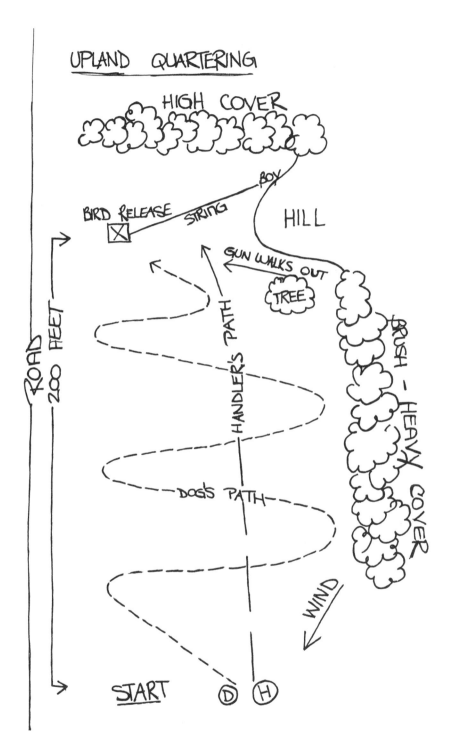

UPLAND QUARTERING

HIGH COVER

HILL

BOY

BIRD RELEASE   STRING

ROAD
200 FEET

GUN WALKS OUT

TREE

HANDLER'S PATH

DOG'S PATH

BRUSH - HEAVY COVER

WIND

START   D   H

A WATER TEST

This typical water test simulates a real hunter's problem (see diagram). The hunter sits on a stool behind a blind. The dog is commanded to SIT outside the blind about 8 feet from the hunter. The dog is in a position to see all the action and is required to SIT and STAY (without the handler next to him) until all the action is over. First, about 80 yards away, a shot is fired by a hidden gun, but there is no evidence of a bird. (In this case the dog is responsible for handling birds downed by guns in two blinds, his own and the one 80 yards away. The distant first shot will provide the opportunity for a blind retrieve.) Next, two shots are fired form the handler's blind and two shackled ducks are thrown from behind the reeds to points X1 and X2. The dog sees the birds in the air but cannot see them once they hit the water behind the reeds. The handler then sends the dog for the last bird down and after that for the other bird behind the tules. These two birds simulate a double made from the handler's blind. Then the dog is sent to point X to make the blind retrieve.

That test can be set up for all the dogs but is simplified for the younger ones. This is where the judges must have experience. The double retrieve can be made into two single retrieves, and the blind can be shortened for intermediate dogs or make into a single retrieve for juniors. In the Hunting Retriever Stake the idea is to have all the dogs do the best they can and not be eliminated, so they can get in as much work as possible. It is hoped that the older, better trained dogs will set an example for the less experienced handlers . . . that's how we shall get better hunting work from the dogs.

This stake offers a way for the hunter to learn and to see other people's dogs work, and for his dog, too, to get a learning experience. All will benefit. It makes a great tune-up for an upcoming hunting season, and provides fun, training, and good sport after the season. It will afford a way to evaluate hunting retrievers, and future pups should be pleased about that.

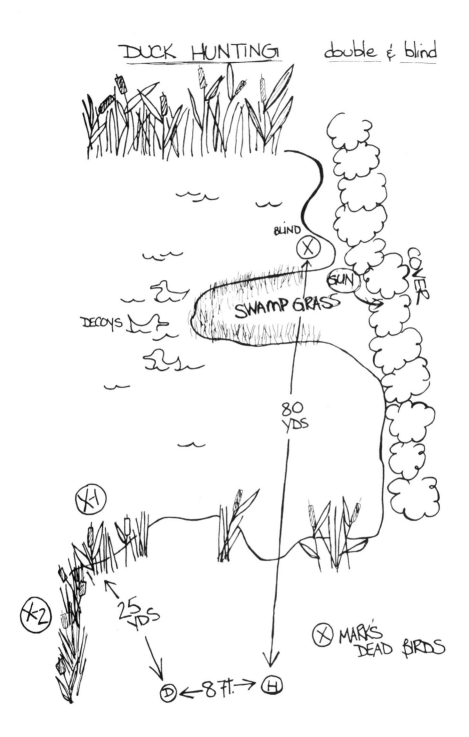

DUCK HUNTING

double & blind

BLIND

SUN

COVER

SWAMP GRASS

DECOYS

80 YDS

X-1

X-2

25 YDS

Ⓧ MARK'S DEAD BIRDS

Ⓓ ←— 8 ft. —→ Ⓗ

THAT'S THE BOOK

Except for Gene Hill, who follows this, and Appendixes I and II, that's the end of the book. If you have followed our game plan, at eight to ten months of age, or even make it a year, your dog will retrieve, handle, and hunt upland game. He is ready to go anywhere and do a job that will have your cronies dropping their jaws in amazement. By this time you should have instilled two qualities into your retriever—control and desire.

We have shown you how to get the control. Let me end by saying once again that the commands SIT, STAY, and COME are the bases of the whole game. If your dog has those three commands down pat, whether at heel or 100 yards away, you will be able to teach the dog all the other work. It has been a logical, natural procedure, with minimum force. It has been fast and directed toward the hunter's needs. If your dog does not respond smartly to these basic commands, in all situations, you will get into trouble. It is that simple.

As for desire, we have shown you how to bring out the best and develop what the pup's mom and pop "built into" him. Remember, we cannot teach a dog *to* hunt but only teach him *how* to hunt. If you are convinced that the retrieving and game-finding desires are not there, there is nothing you can do about that. With good breeding it practically never happens, if you start early with the pup. It will happen more often if training is put off.

We have tried to be logical and consistent with you in taking you through this training method step by step. If you will do the same with your pup, your success is guaranteed. If you have developed in your dog the control and desire that I say you can have at this early age, what do you think your dog will be like with two or three years of experience in hunting with you?

Training a dog to do his job with style is like creating a work of art. To paint a scene or turn a piece of stone into something others admire is a real accomplishment. How proud I am of young Tar.

The end

Epilogue

An *epilogue* was most common as a speech after a conclusion of a Greek play. It gave the audience something else to think about. There is nothing I can add to Dick's training lessons, per se, but I can speak about the validity of both their purpose and their results.

Some time ago I trained and ran a couple of pretty good dogs in field trials. I also used the same dogs for upland hunting (and in lieu of an electric blanket until they started imitating my snoring). The point being that a good dog is too valuable, and much too intelligent, not to use it to do everything within the full range of its capabilities. I shoot my "best" guns in the field as well as in competition; why not ask as much of a "best" dog?

Dick did not dwell much on the aesthetics of his subject, so I think I ought to touch on that, because in many ways the art or beauty of hunting is largely tied in with the satisfaction and associations that come about with our use of the dog. I enjoyed my successes as a retriever trainer more than my questionable ability as a wingshot—and the better I trained the less I had to work on my left-to-right crossing shots! In fact, most of the time I preferred working my dogs to doing the shooting. I strongly suspect that many of you will find yourselves feeling the exact same way when your work with your dog reaches that stage where you want to see just how fine a polish you can get—and you'll be very pleasantly surprised in most cases. As for game conservation, the value of a well-trained retriever is too obvious to be dwelled on at length. The satisfaction you'll derive from bagging many birds that would otherwise be lost is very deep indeed.

I see no harm in looking at a well- and successfully hunted field or a fine day's gunning in a waterfowl blind as a "play." The actors have performed their roles well, and the drama has had a happy ending. The epilogue, in its ancient tradition, has me telling you that this is the way things ought to be done. The man and the dog have worked hard and pleasurably together to have it come out just so. They are both rightly pleased with themselves, and should you wish to be the same—all you have to do is learn your part.

This play is really what hunting is all about. Hidden away in the satisfaction of solving the not-so-difficult problems of finding a bird and bringing it to the bag are the timeless delights that only the hunter and his dog can know. I have often felt the urge to applaud when I've seen the act work well—and I'm sure that I must have done so, although probably not often enough.

There are, on second thought, a couple of things that Dick doesn't tell you. You're going to feel angry, often. And frustrated ... and the urge to beat yourself and the dog will be overwhelming; just when you think you've got a handle on something, it will all unravel. Well, it's happened to me—and to Dick and to lots of our dogs. But stick with it. In the not-too-long run something will start to work just the way it should, and then something else and something else. Part of it will be a better dog and no less a part will be a better hunter. That much I surely promise you.

When a man is proud of his dog and shows it, I like him. When his dog is proud of him and shows it, I deeply respect him.

GENE HILL
Associate Editor
Field and Stream

194

Appendix I

North American Hunting Retriever Association
General Regulations for Hunting Retriever Field Tests

These regulations apply to all categories. **Note:** The passages enclosed in parentheses are guidelines for judges.

Section 1. The term *dog* includes male and female dogs.

Section 2. Once it is determined that a dog is eligible to participate, its eligibility for a particular event is determined by its ability, not age.

Section 3. All tests shall be judged by at least two judges. The judges shall set up all tests within the prescribed guidelines set forth in the Regulations and Field Procedures and shall give paramount consideration to the simulation of actual hunting conditions. In keeping with this aim:

a. All tests shall be set up within reasonable hunting distances in open to heavy cover.

b. Duck blinds, numerous decoys, boats, calls, and other hunting implements shall be utilized.

c. Judges shall decide on the placement of gunners and bird boys.

d. Handlers, bird boys, gunners, judges, and others shall be required to wear camouflage or dark clothing. Clubs hosting licensed Field Tests should be prepared to provide an appropriate covering for participating persons who do not come to the event with such clothing.

e. Events shall utilize live or dead pheasants, pigeons, ducks, or other game birds.

Section 4. Voice or whistle commands shall be allowed to steady the dog at the point of origin. However, voice or whistle commands that are excessive, in the opinion of the judges, shall be marked down.

Section 6. When at the point of origin, the handler shall not possess any exposed training aid that might intimidate the dog (including, but not limited to, leash, lead, whip, quirt, cane, prod, or similar implements) or indulge in any behavior that may in any way intimidate the dog. A Started dog only may have a collar, leash, or line around its neck or may be hand-held by one hand to assist in achieving steadiness.

Section 7. The judges of a particular category shall have the authority to expel a handler from any further participation in that category if they observe unsportsmanlike conduct on the part of the handler or see the handler kicking, striking, or otherwise manhandling a dog while on the Field Test grounds or while the judging of the category is in process. It will be the duty of the judges promptly to report to the

Field Test Committee the expulsion of a handler from a category, and the Field Test Committee may then expel the handler from all other categories at that event, if in the committee's opinion, such further action is warranted. Whenever a handler is expelled from a category or from participation at a Field Test under this Section, the dog or dogs that he is handling may continue to be tested with another handler.

The Field Test Secretary shall submit to NAHRA a complete report of any action taken under this Section by either the Field Test Committee or the judges.

Section 8. Dogs requiring help from the bird boys shall be disqualified. Stone or object throwing shall not be allowed.

Section 9. Incidents of intentional hardmouth resulting, in the opinion of the judges, in a bird unfit for the table shall be grounds for failing a test.

(Hardmouth is difficult to prove. If the judges observe that a dog is hardmouthing, but not to a degree calling for failure, the judges may penalize the dog for bad manners. A dog that drops a bird more than is necessary to get a better grip on it shall be marked down. The dog should pick up a bird tenderly but firmly, and most important, without hesitation and with dispatch. Hovering over a bird shall be marked down. The dog should not drop a bird for any reason except to get a better grip; a dog that drops a bird to shake shall be marked down; a dog that drops a bird to relieve itself shall be marked down.)

Section 10. Bitches in season shall not be permitted on the test grounds.

Section 11. All persons participating in or observing any event are expected to maintain reasonable silence and display good manners. Any person who interferes with the orderly process of any test may be obliged by the Field Test Committee to leave the test grounds.

Section 12. The judges shall follow the Regulations and Field Procedures and the Guidelines for Judging Hunting Retriever Field Tests in all tests.

Section 13. Prior to the start of each test, the judges shall explain to the handlers the hunting scenario and object of each test and expected performance of the dogs. Any questions by handlers shall be voiced prior to the running of each test.

(NAHRA's purpose in establishing these General Regulations and Field Procedures is to discover and reward dogs that can fulfill the hunter's needs in the field while performing in a manner consistent with the demands of actual hunting conditions. Tests will be designed to simulate a day's hunting afield. The purpose is not to confront the dog with artificial or trick problems, but rather to test the dog's natural ability and training.)

Section 14. A *test* shall be defined for these purposes as: The evaluation of a dog as required by the Regulations and Field Procedures and during which the dog is being scored.

Section 15. A judge shall not be requested nor be required to place dogs in order of finish, nor shall the judges place dogs in order of finish.

Section 16. A judge shall not be requested nor required to discuss his or her judging evaluations with any participant. The decision of the judges shall be final.

Section 17. Upon receipt of an application therefor, NAHRA may license or approve its properly affiliated clubs to hold Beginner events for all dogs. Such events shall be held in conjunction with licensed or approved NAHRA Hunting Retriever Field Tests.

A request for a Beginner event must be made on the Field Test Application. Entries shall not be limited, and any dog may participate. NAHRA shall keep no records of the events. Each club hosting a licensed or approved Beginner event within fifteen (15) days of the end of the event shall report to NAHRA, on its Field Test Report, the number of dogs entered and actually run and shall pay to NAHRA the sum of $.50 for each dog actually run in such an event. Judges for a Beginner event need not be certified or accredited by NAHRA.

Each club shall establish its own rules by which dogs shall be judged in this informal event. However, under no circumstances shall the rules be as restrictive as the requirements or the regulations governing Started Hunting Retrievers, nor shall they exceed those requirements.

No club shall advertise a Beginner event as a hunting retriever event or field test. Dogs successfully completing a NAHRA Beginner event shall be awarded a NAHRA Certificate of Merit. Certificates of Merit shall be purchased by clubs from NAHRA.

REGULATIONS AND FIELD PROCEDURES FOR STARTED™ HUNTING RETRIEVER FIELD TEST

Section 1. A Started Hunting Retriever Field Test shall consist of only five (5) single bird marking tests at least two of which shall be marked water retrieves and at least two of which shall be marked land retrieves. The fifth marked retrieve may be on either land or water.

(The purpose of the Started Hunting Retriever Field Test is to bring young or Started dogs along as hunters. Desire and cooperation with the handler are important factors. It should consist of simple tests to evaluate the dog's natural ability.)

Section 2. A dog is required to be steady at the point of origin; however, it may have a collar, leash, or line around its neck and/or may be hand-held by one hand only to assist in achieving steadiness. A controlled break shall not fail a dog but shall be marked down. (As soon as the dog leaves the point of origin and manifests an intent to make the retrieve without being so ordered, it must be stopped. If a dog is immediately brought under control, it shall be considered a controlled break, which is a minor infraction.)

(The judges should evaluate the dog's temperament, as displayed in its spontaneous behavior, in order to assess its suitability as a hunting companion. Hyperactivity, wildness, jumping about, barking, excessive disobedience, lethargy, or lack of interest shall be marked down.)

Section 3. A dog is not required to deliver to hand, but must deliver the bird back into a prearranged delivery area.

(The dog should return to the handler without undue delay.)

Section 4. A dog may be urged to hunt by voice, whistle, or hand signals, but shall be marked down if the voice, whistle, or hand signals are, in the opinion c judges, excessive.

Section 5. A dog may be cast from the point of origin no more than twice. (ı. the dog is recast it shall be marked down. After two [2] unsuccessful attempts, the judges shall step in and direct the handler to pick up his/her dog.)

Section 6. Tests for this event shall be held in appropriate light to medium cover.

    a. Maximum test distance on land shall not exceed approximately 75 yards.

    b. Maximum test distance on water shall not exceed approximately 50 yards.

    c. Dogs shall not be required to honor another dog in this event.

    d. Dry shots (i.e., shots for which no bird appears or falls) or game calls may be used as diversions. However, no additional birds shall be used as diversions.

Section 7. Hidden gunners and bird boys shall be used unless they are at the point of origin. From the area from which the bird is to appear, an attention-getting attraction shot or shots shall be fired or a game call shall be blown prior to the bird's being thrown, and additionally, a shot shall be fired when the bird is at the top of its arc. At the discretion of the judges, not more than once in each event, the gunners may be visible in order to simulate specific hunting situations such as dove hunting. (It is the intent of these Regulations to provide the dog with adequate opportunity to focus its attention on the area of the fall.)

REGULATIONS AND FIELD PROCEDURES FOR INTERMEDIATE™ HUNTING RETRIEVER FIELD TESTS™

Section 1. An Intermediate Field Test shall consist of five (5) tests, which shall include the following: Quartering; a blind retrieve on water that shall not be incorporated in another test; a double marked land retrieve; a double marked water retrieve; and trailing.

(The purpose of Intermediate Hunting Retriever Tests is to bring working dogs to a higher standard of performance. Desire and teamwork with the handler are important factors. They shall consist of tests that enable the judges to evaluate natural ability and handler control.)

Section 2. A dog shall be steady at the point of origin (see paragraph b of this section).

    a. A dog may be touched or patted at the point of origin to steady, but once the "ready" signal has been given to the judges by the handler, the dog may not be touched again.

    b. A controlled break shall not fail a dog, but it shall be marked down.

(For marks, the point of origin is the point at which the dog is located at the time the first bird becomes visible.)

(As soon as the dog leaves the point of origin and manifests an intent to make the retrieve without being so ordered, it must be stopped. If a dog is immediately brought under control, it shall be considered a minor infraction.)

Section 3. A dog shall deliver all birds to hand. (The dog should return to the handler without undue delay.)

Section 4. On marked retrieves or blind retrieves, a dog may be handled by voice/whistle commands and/or hand signals or urged to hunt, but shall be marked down if the voice, whistle, or hand signals are, in the opinion of the judges, excessive, unless a special test regulation or procedure specifies differently, such as trailing after a mark.

Section 5. A dog may be cast from the point of origin only once.

(If the attempt is unsuccessful, the judges shall step in and direct the handler to pick up his/her dog. However, if in the judges' opinion, the dog exhibits confusion at the point of origin, the judges may allow a recast. The judges must signal for a recast before the dog leaves the immediate area of the point of origin.)

Section 6. Tests in this event shall be held in appropriate cover.
  a. Maximum test distance on land shall not exceed approximately 100 yards.
  b. Maximum test distance on water shall not exceed approximately 75 yards.

Section 7. Walk-ups to simulate jump shooting may be used in this event. The dog shall be brought to an area designated as the point of origin at heel or under control approximately ten (10) feet in front of the handler. Section 2b shall be in effect. The judges shall signal for the bird while the handler and dog are walking.

Section 8. Hidden gunners and bird boys shall be used unless they are at the point of origin. From the area from which the bird is to appear, an attention-getting attraction shot or shots shall be fired or game call blown prior to each bird's being thrown. A shot or shots shall be fired when the bird is at the top of its arc. At the discretion of the judges but not more than once in each event, the gunners may be visible in order to simulate specific hunting situations such as dove hunting. (It is the intent of these Regulations to provide the dog with an adequate opportunity to focus its attention on the area of the fall.)

Section 9. Dry shots may be fired. (A *dry shot* is defined as a shot for which no bird is thrown or appears.) Game calls and additional birds with or without shots may also be used as diversions as a dog returns from a retrieve. A dog that does switch shall not be failed but shall be marked down.

Section 10. The handler may be required to handle an empty shotgun with both hands on the firearm in the firing position.

Section 11. Tests for this event shall normally consist of double retrieves on both land and water.
  a. The handler shall not point out the location of the gunners and bird boys to the dog prior to the time the bird is thrown. (A violation of this subsection is a major infraction and shall result in the dog being marked down.)
  b. Triple marks shall not be used.
  c. Dogs shall not be required to honor another dog.

Section 12. Blind retrieves on water only shall be used in this event, but shall not exceed thirty (30) yards in length through appropriate cover. Dogs may be cast from the point of origin only once (see Section 5 above regarding confusion).
  a. A diversionary bird may be thrown and guns or dry shots fired as the dog

returns. A dog that drops a bird shall not be failed, but shall be severely marked down.

b. Simultaneous falls with birds and shots originating from the same location may be used.

c. A quartering test shall be used. The dog shall be required to quarter as in upland hunting within gun range of the handler. A dog may be urged to hunt or handled by hand, voice, or whistle commands; however, voice/whistle commands that are, in the opinion of the judges, excessive shall be marked down. (At the discretion of the judges, the dog may be required to locate a dead bird or birds.)

d. A trailing test shall be used. The dog shall be required to trail and locate a bird. The dog shall be scored on its natural ability and its use of its nose to locate and follow the trail. A dog may be urged to hunt by voice/whistle commands; however, voice/whistle commands that are, in the opinion of the judges, excessive shall be marked down. (Judges shall restrict entry of the handlers into the area of the trail. Hand signals are inappropriate and shall not be used other than to put the dog onto the beginning of the trail.)

e. Retrieves simulating cripple retrieves may be used.

f. Dogs may be required to be placed at a point of origin at a distance from the handler.

g. Portions of tests may be established that gauge a dog's ability and suitability as a hunting retriever which may not require the dog to make a retrieve. Such tests may include, but are not limited to, fly-aways, and a test simulating the placement and pickup of decoys using a boat or canoe.

REGULATIONS AND FIELD PROCEDURES FOR SENIOR™ HUNTING RETRIEVER FIELD TESTS™

Section 1. A Senior Field Test shall consist of at least six (6) tests, which shall include the following: a multiple marked water retrieve; a multiple marked land retrieve; quartering (which shall not be considered a marked retrieve); trailing; a water blind retrieve, and a land blind retrieve, at least one of which shall be incorporated within one of the required multiple marked retrieves.

(The Senior Hunting Retriever Test is for the finished dog; the Started and Intermediate events are intended primarily for training and experience. The judging of these tests should be relaxed and helpful to the dog and the handler. The Senior Field Test must consist of serious tests worthy of the hunter's retriever. The making of a Master Hunting Retriever [MHR] is a serious responsibility. The dogs should be tested on their natural ability and training accomplishments. Simply completing a test will not be enough; the tests must be completed with style and precision.)

Section 2. A dog shall be steady at the point of origin (see subparagraph c of this Section). (For marks, the point of origin is the point at which the dog is located at the time the first bird becomes visible.)

a. Voice/whistle commands shall be allowed to steady a dog at the point of origin.

b. A dog may be touched or patted at the point of origin to steady, but once the "ready" signal has been given to the judges by the handler, the dog may not be touched again.

c. A controlled break shall not fail a dog, but it shall be marked down. (As soon as the dog leaves the point of origin and manifests an intent to make the retrieve without being so ordered, it must be stopped. If a dog is immediately brought under control, it shall be considered a minor infraction.)

Section 3. A dog shall deliver all birds to hand.

Section 4. On marked retrieves, a dog may be handled by voice/whistle and/or hand signals or urged to hunt by voice command, but shall be marked down.

(The dog is being tested for its marking ability, not handling; however, a crisp handle is preferable to a long hunt.)

Section 5. A dog shall be cast from the point of origin a maximum of once. (If, in the opinion of the judges, the dog exhibits confusion at the point of origin, the judges may allow a recast; however, the judges must signal for a recast before the dog leaves the immediate area of the point of origin.)

Section 6. Dogs may be required to honor another dog at or near the point of origin during the entire test. An honoring dog's view of the test shall not be obstructed.

Section 7. Maximum test distance for land or water marks shall not exceed approximately one hundred (100) yards.

Section 8. Tests for this event shall normally consist of double marks on both water and land, and dogs may be required to make retrieves in a sequence established by the judges. The handler shall not point out the location of the gunners or bird boys to the dog prior to the time the bird is thrown.

a. Triple marks may be used.

b. Blind retrieves on water and land shall be used. Maximum distances shall not exceed approximately one hundred (100) yards.

(Handling in these tests must be done with precision. The dog must stop on whistle. Judges should look for perseverance, obedience, and style. A cast refusal may be a serious infraction. The judges must decide on the seriousness of the refusal by taking into account the conditions at hand.)

c. A diversionary bird or birds may be thrown and guns or dry shots fired. The order and sequence of the retrieve shall be determined by the judges.

d. Walk-ups to simulate jump shooting may be used in this event. The dog shall be brought to an area designated as the point of origin at heel or under control approximately ten (10) feet in front of the handler. Section 2, paragraphs a, b, and c shall be in effect. The judges shall signal for the bird while the handler and dog are walking.

e. Hidden gunners and bird boys shall be used in this event unless they are at the point of origin. From the area from which the bird is to appear, an attention-getting attraction shot or shots shall be fired or game call blown prior to each bird's being thrown. A shot or shots shall be fired when each bird is at the top of its arc. At the discretion of the judges, but not more than once for any one dog, the gunners may be visible in order to simulate specific hunting situations such as dove hunting. (It is the intent of these Regulations to provide the dog with an adequate opportunity to focus its attention on the area of the fall.)

f. Dogs may be required to be placed at the point of origin at a distance from the handler.

g. The handler may be required to handle an empty shotgun with both hands on the firearm in the firing position.

h. Simultaneous falls with birds and shots originating from the same location may be used.

i. Delayed marks or falls may be used.

j. Quartering tests shall be used. A live bird or birds shall be utilized. The dog shall be required to retrieve to hand. The retrieve shall not be scored as a mark, but it must be completed. The dog shall be required to quarter and locate birds as in upland hunting within gun range of the handler. A dog may be urged to hunt or handled by hand/voice/whistle commands; however, hand/voice/whistle commands that are, in the opinion of the judges, excessive shall be marked down. A dog shall be steady to wing and shall be disqualified if it is not. A dog shall be steady to shot and fall, and shall be disqualified if it is not. If a dog is manifesting an intent to chase or catch the bird at the time that the shot is fired or at the time that, in the judges' opinion, the shot should have been fired, then the dog is not steady to wing. If a dog is steady to wing but then breaks at the shot and manifests an intent to make the retrieve without being so ordered, it must be stopped. If a dog is immediately stopped and brought under control, it shall be considered a minor infraction.)

k. Trailing tests shall be used. The dog shall be required to trail and locate a bird. The dog shall be scored on its natural ability and its use of its nose to locate and follow the trail of the bird. A dog may be urged to hunt or handled by hand/voice/whistle commands; however, hand/voice/whistle commands that are, in the opinion of the judges, excessive shall be marked down. (Judges shall restrict entry of the handlers into the area of the trail. Hand signals are inappropriate and shall not be used other than to put the dog onto the beginning of the trail.)

l. Retrieves simulating crippled retrieves may be used.

m. Tests may be established, which gauge the dog's ability and suitability as a hunting retriever, that may not require the dog to retrieve. Such tests shall include, but are not limited to, fly-aways, tests simulating the placement and pickup of decoys using a boat or canoe, tests designed to gauge a dog's control or suitability as a hunting retriever where retrieves are made from a neighboring blind by another dog, or tests in which the dog is required to remain stationary at a distance from the handler.

(**Note:** Readers wishing to obtain the complete booklet of rules and regulations of the North American Hunting Retriever Association, including "General Procedures" and the complete "Guidelines for Judging NAHRA Hunting Retriever Field Tests," should write to North American Hunting Retriever Association, Inc., P.O. Box 6, Garrisonville, VA 22463.)

Appendix II

A Dog's Mental Development: The Five Critical Periods*

This outline of the five critical stages in a dog's mental development is based on the findings of Dr. J. Paul Scott and his team of researchers at the Animal Behavior Laboratory at Hamilton Station, which is a part of the Roscoe B. Jackson Memorial Laboratory on Mount Desert Island, Maine. Dr. Scott's work was done in conjunction with Guide Dogs for the Blind, Inc., in a highly successful program to accelerate the training of Seeing-Eye Dogs for the blind. By starting to train pups at the 49th day instead of waiting for them to grow up, the experimenters raised the success rate for producing qualified Guide Dogs from 20 percent to more than 90 percent.

FIRST CRITICAL PERIOD—0 TO 21 DAYS

Zero to 21 days is the first critical period. During these three weeks the pup's mental capacity is almost zero. The pup reacts only to his needs—warmth, food, sleep, and its mother. If anything at all could be taught, it would be strictly in the area of survival, such as a simple test of getting food. Abruptly on the 21st day his senses seem to function. He's like a house that's been built and wired for all the electrical appliances but has not been hooked up to the current. Then on the specific day the juice is applied and everything starts to function. In all breeds of dogs this happens on the 21st day of life. This leads immediately to the second critical period.

SECOND CRITICAL PERIOD—21 to 28 DAYS

The 21st to the 28th day is the time of the second phase—it's when the pup absolutely needs Momma. During this week the dog's senses function, the brain and nervous system start to develop, and the big new world around him can be a pretty frightening experience. The emotional and social stress of life will have the greatest impact on him during this week. Removal from mother at this time could be catastrophic.

THIRD CRITICAL PERIOD—28 TO 49 DAYS

From 28 to 49 days is the third period of development. Slowly the dog reacts to his surroundings. He ventures away from Mother to explore the world around him. It's at the end of this period that the dog's nervous system

*From *Water Dog*, Richard A. Wolters, Dutton, 1964.

and his brain will have developed to the capacity of an adult but, of course, without the experience. He'll be ready to recognize people and respond to the voice. He'll have spent enough time in the litter to know that he's a dog. This may sound strange, but it has been shown that puppies taken from the litter too soon were difficult to breed later on. They just never got the idea that they were dogs. It's also during this third period that the social order or pecking order of the litter starts to form. This means the pups that learn to get in and fight for their food will tend to become bullies and the pups that are cowed by the more aggressive pups will become shy and develop wallflower personalities. It's desirable for the pup to live in the litter long enough for him to get a little competitive spirit from his family life, but too much is harmful. The puppy is now ready to learn, and learn he will; so it's better for you to get into the picture at this point and have him learn the things that will mold the type of personality that you want the dog to have.

Up until this time the dog was too young to take from the mother, and does benefit from the social situation of the litter. But when *the dog is exactly 49 days old,* although he will be physically immature, his brain will have attained its full adult form.

FOURTH CRITICAL PERIOD—49 to 84 DAYS

The trainer and the dog should start to get to know each other *now,* not a week later or a week earlier. Dr. Scott's research has shown that this, the 49th day, is the best time in a dog's life to establish the dog-human relationship. The person who's going to train the dog will, in effect, now take the place of the pup's mother. Through feeding, playing, and general care of the dog at this age—seven to twelve weeks—a bond will be established that will have a permanent effect on the dog. At no later time in the dog's life will the pup have the ability to achieve as strong a bond or rapport with humans as at this age.

The research at the Behavior Laboratory showed that human contact in this seven- to twelve-week period is almost the whole key to the dog's future prospects. Puppies that were completely isolated for as little as the first sixteen weeks of life grew into dogs that were incapable of being trained, let alone becoming companion dogs.

Simple commands can be taught at this time. The teaching is at this point in the form of games. There should be no discipline, and by the time the dog is twelve weeks old—the end of the preschool or fourth critical stage of his development—the dog will know what is meant by commands SIT, STAY, COME, and possibly HEEL.

Getting settled in the new home is a very important part of his education. A secure puppy will be a happy dog and will take to learning and discipline.

The new information has shown that dogs can get what is called kennel blindness. They just eat and sleep and exist, waiting for someone to come and plunk down some money in order to take them home. Dogs that have had absolutely no human contact before sixteen weeks of age have little chance of becoming what we want in a companion. Dogs that have missed human contact for even thirteen weeks, and who were bred to become working dogs, may be completely untrainable as workers.

One of the most interesting aspects of the Seeing-Eye research was the information about interrupted training. Dogs started at a very early age, handled and trained through this fourth critical period—age twelve weeks —were then put back in the kennel situation. The lessons stopped for a period of only two weeks. After the two weeks, human contact and lessons were begun again, but only 57 percent of these dogs were able to go on to become Guide Dogs. When the formal lessons and human contact were stopped for three weeks, only 30 percent went on through the rigorous training to become guides. These facts dramatically show that to make the most of a dog, the training has to begin early and without interruption and be carried into the last critical phase of the puppy's development.

FIFTH CRITICAL PERIOD—84 to 112 DAYS

This fifth period—from 12 to 16 weeks—is when the puppy starts to school. The play-teaching games stop and the formal lessons start. The dog is ready to learn *disciplined* behavior. This is the time a young dog will declare his independence. At this time, dog and trainer resolve the problem of who's going to be boss. Deciding who's boss can be settled if the dog is started late, but it might take a two-by-four to do it.

We prepare the dog for learning in the seven- to twelve-week period. Fundamental training then begins at twelve weeks, and by the end of sixteen weeks this dog will know his basic commands and respond well to them.

This information is the same for all breeds, pure bred or not. I've heard handlers say that they started their dog at a year and have had fine results. What they don't know is how much better their dog could have been if the bond between teacher and student was made early. A child or dog that has a good early experience learning will enjoy learning, and they will learn to learn.

INDEX